Rapid Graphs with Tableau 8

The Original Guide for the Accidental Analyst

Stephen McDaniel

Director of Analytics, **Tableau Software**®
Principal Data Scientist, **Freakalytics**®, **LLC**

Eileen McDaniel, Ph.D.

Managing Partner, **Freakalytics, LLC**

Technical Reviewer: **Marc Rueter**
Senior Director of Technology, Consulting and Strategy
Tableau Software

Current Cover Design: **Stephen McDaniel**
Original Cover Design: **Cristy Miller**

Cover graphs and page made in Tableau by Stephen McDaniel
with original version feedback by Ellie Fields and Chris Stolte of Tableau Software

Please visit us at <u>Freakalytics.com</u>

At Freakalytics we offer dynamic, live training in the techniques and tools needed to discover the value long hidden in your data. Our training is designed with one goal in mind—to empower you to make informed decisions and achieve success in your daily work.

As an independent two-person advisory and training firm, you can seek advice and attend our training knowing that we speak freely about the pros and cons of various tools, techniques and approaches. We typically work with clients on short-term strategic projects that kick-start new analytics initiatives or provide guidance for client teams that instill confidence with a clear plan for success.

Stephen is recognized as one of the top Tableau users in the world. After writing **SAS for Dummies**, Stephen approached executives at Tableau in 2008 about writing the first edition of this book. At Tableau headquarters, Stephen works on developing the future vision of the software. He improved or authored the sample dashboards, analyses and data sources that are included with every Tableau 8 install. These five sample workbooks are included at the bottom of Tableau Desktop home page. Specifically, Stephen was lead author of the entire World indicators workbook, Economic Indicators in the Finance workbook, Growth of Wal-Mart and Simple Forecasting in the Sales workbook, and Nuclear Power Plants in the Variety workbook. Additionally, Stephen compiled and prepared the World Bank Indicators data source (home page, upper left).

Please check our website for information on our new book and training program, **The Accidental Analyst: Show Your Data Who's Boss**, written for people who didn't plan for careers in data analysis, but are now facing mountains of data in their daily work and need a step-by-step plan of how to answer questions and make decisions. The book includes visual analytics best practices and applies to any analytic software, and has been popular among users of many applications. Executives at Tableau were so excited about early drafts of **The Accidental Analyst** that they purchased a pre-publication copy for every attendee of their Customer Conference in Las Vegas in October of 2011.

Thanks to our public and on-site seminar attendees!
We have enjoyed helping you overcome your data challenges and we still learn something new in every class we teach!

Table of Contents

Chapter 1

Analyzing your data for success at work

Quickly answer your business questions and communicate your results

In today's world, we are all trying to make sense of the mountains of data that we encounter in our jobs every day, whether we work in business, information technology, government, education, research, or for a non-profit organization. We would like to obtain answers quickly and easily from our data, so that we can increase our productivity and make informed decisions about what actions to take. Our mission is to help people find these answers and communicate them effectively, whether you are new to analysis or have been analyzing data for years. This book, now in its fourth edition, can teach you how to achieve these goals with a case study approach using Tableau Software as the tool.

Would you like to be able to…

- Quickly build tables and graphs using the best practices of visual analytics to answer simple questions about your data?

- Answer complex questions about your data with little or no programming?

- Change your tables and graphs on the spot to look how you want, just by clicking on them?

- Create attractive and interactive presentations that not only inform your colleagues, but keep them interested and engaged in what you have to say?

- Allow the software to guide you in your analysis or hand you total control, depending on what you need?

The information in this book can empower you to accomplish this and more. Even if you are new to data analysis, you can learn the basics and possibly some advanced features in a short amount of time if you follow the hands-on exercises.

Stephen approached the executives at Tableau with the idea of writing the first book on Tableau in 2008. After completing that version for Tableau 5, we were inspired to develop Tableau's initial training program in 2009 as the founding Tableau Education Partner. As a small independent company, we authored the original courses and taught students around the world, both in our own workshops and at Tableau Customer Conferences. Although Tableau is a much larger company than it was back in those days, we still teach our own workshops! Our students have been successful with our approach, in which people learn how to analyze their data first and foremost, with software as the tool, and we are passionate about what we do.

In this book, you will learn the five ways that Tableau can help you to be a better a data analyst: power, speed, flexibility, simplicity and beauty. Take a look at the following examples to see what is possible!

Power

Whether you are exploring your data for new insights, answering specific questions or even deciding what questions to ask, learn how to investigate, communicate and take action with the valuable information hidden in your data! There are a wide variety of options to graph your data using best practices, the ability to adjust your data so that you are using the right data in the right form for the questions at hand. You can work with every major data source, from Excel workbooks to the largest databases. You can even extract data from larger sources into a local "extract" file that will make your data exploration more efficient and allow offline analysis when you are away from the office.

Profit and *planned profit* by *product*
Dark bars are below plan, light bars are above plan
Percentage is above/below plan
Black line is the planned profit amount

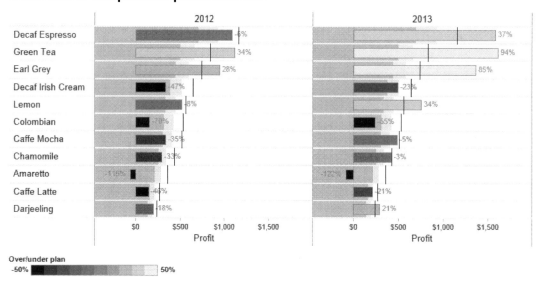

Displaying *profit* versus *sales* by *region* and *customer segment*
Bubble size is average profit ratio
Minimum and maximum profit ratios labeled per region
Colors are *customer segments*

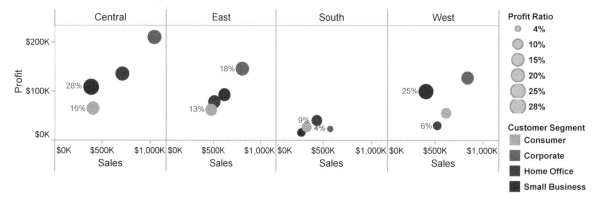

Exploring the relationship of *profit* to *sales* by *region*
Each point in the graph is a customer order
Colors are *customer segments*
A trend line is displayed for each *customer segment* per *region*

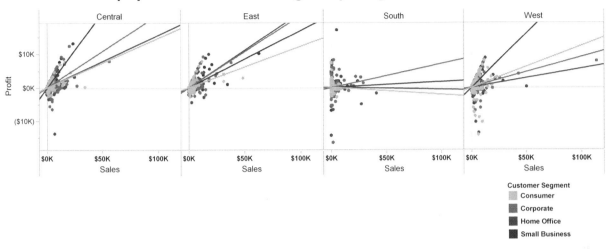

Map of per-capita income growth, 2006 to 2008
Color and size of bubble are growth rates (the darker and larger, the better)
Labeled states have the highest and lowest growth rates

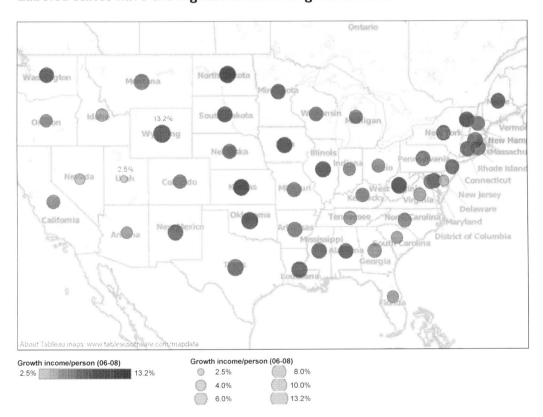

Scatter plot of per-capita income growth by region, 2006 to 2008
Colors are income growth (the darker the better)
Reference lines are median values for each region
Labeled states are top and bottom for the region

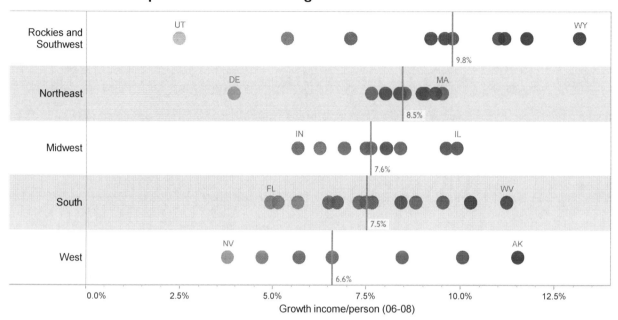

Growth income/person (06-08)

2.5%   13.2%

Speed

Faster than you thought possible, you will learn how to build presentation quality graphs and tables. You can have total control over creating the view or you have a view generated automatically based on the data that you select. From the view, you can rapidly sort, filter and group the displayed data—with just a few clicks of your mouse. Each example demonstrates rapid changes made in just a few seconds!

Sales and *profit ratio* by zip code—
from bar chart to map with one click!

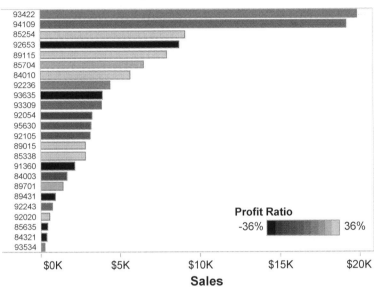

Highlight a data point to quickly examine the values behind it

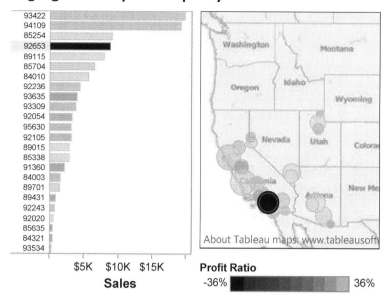

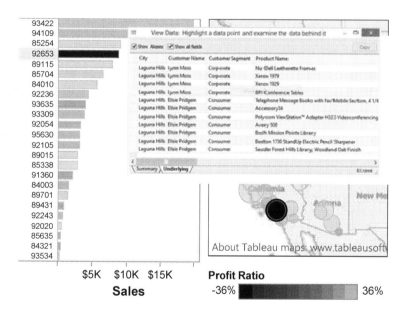

Four views are better than one:
From detailed table to color-highlighted table to
side-by-side bar chart to color-encoded bar chart!

		Profit								Over/under plan							
		2012				2013				2012				2013			
		Q1	Q2	Q3	Q4	Q1	Q2	Q3	Q4	Q1	Q2	Q3	Q4	Q1	Q2	Q3	Q4
Central	Coffee	$2,208	$2,473	$2,560	$2,249	$3,330	$3,492	$3,611	$3,341	-22%	-20%	-20%	-24%	18%	12%	13%	12%
	Espresso	$2,369	$2,457	$2,481	$2,271	$3,570	$3,477	$3,506	$3,370	-28%	-27%	-29%	-45%	8%	4%	1%	-18%
	Herbal Tea	$2,414	$2,579	$2,648	$2,450	$3,642	$3,647	$3,738	$3,639	-13%	-12%	-11%	-9%	31%	24%	25%	35%
	Tea	$2,118	$2,317	$2,423	$2,245	$3,195	$3,272	$3,424	$3,336	4%	4%	5%	13%	57%	47%	49%	68%
East	Coffee	$2,747	$3,352	$3,740	$2,817	$4,144	$4,732	$5,278	$4,182	-5%	-4%	-5%	-1%	44%	36%	34%	47%
	Espresso	$562	$610	$372	$990	$848	$863	$530	$1,469	-41%	-43%	-55%	-34%	-12%	-19%	-36%	-2%
	Herbal Tea	$591	$922	$522	$592	$889	$1,306	$725	$876	-23%	-9%	-21%	12%	15%	29%	10%	65%
	Tea	$1,480	$1,615	$1,712	$1,537	$2,229	$2,284	$2,419	$2,282	-22%	-19%	-19%	-20%	18%	15%	14%	19%
South	Coffee	$1,051	$1,198	$1,312	$1,212	$1,585	$1,692	$1,851	$1,801	-39%	-38%	-36%	-41%	-8%	-13%	-10%	-13%
	Espresso	$1,465	$1,540	$1,612	$1,498	$2,209	$2,178	$2,279	$2,224	-11%	-9%	-6%	13%	35%	28%	33%	67%
	Herbal Tea	$561	$529	$591	$669	$843	$749	$837	$992	-31%	-31%	-30%	-28%	4%	-3%	0%	7%
West	Coffee	$1,042	$849	$899	$759	$1,574	$1,201	$1,277	$1,124	-56%	-60%	-60%	-65%	-33%	-44%	-43%	-48%
	Espresso	$2,325	$2,423	$2,540	$2,439	$3,506	$3,429	$3,589	$3,619	-10%	-11%	-10%	-14%	36%	26%	27%	27%
	Herbal Tea	$2,363	$2,739	$2,937	$2,692	$3,566	$3,870	$4,140	$3,996	-10%	-8%	-9%	-6%	36%	30%	28%	40%
	Tea	$1,479	$1,585	$1,630	$1,464	$2,228	$2,237	$2,299	$2,176	4%	8%	3%	22%	57%	52%	46%	81%

	2012				2013			
Product Type	Q1	Q2	Q3	Q4	Q1	Q2	Q3	Q4
Coffee	$7,048	$7,872	$8,511	$7,037	$10,633	$11,117	$12,017	$10,448
Espresso	$6,721	$7,030	$7,005	$7,198	$10,133	$9,947	$9,904	$10,682
Herbal Tea	$5,929	$6,769	$6,698	$6,403	$8,940	$9,572	$9,440	$9,503
Tea	$5,077	$5,517	$5,765	$5,246	$7,652	$7,793	$8,142	$7,794

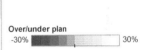

Over/under plan
-30% ▮▮▮▮ 30%

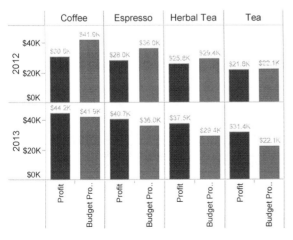

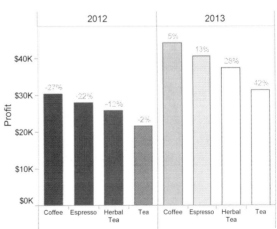

Flexibility

You can easily change any part of your view to look exactly how you want, ranging from data, point shapes and colors to clear data labels to the way your metrics are calculated and compared.

Grouping the data with just a few clicks, from the view

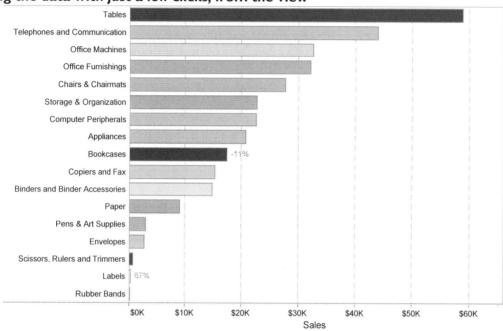

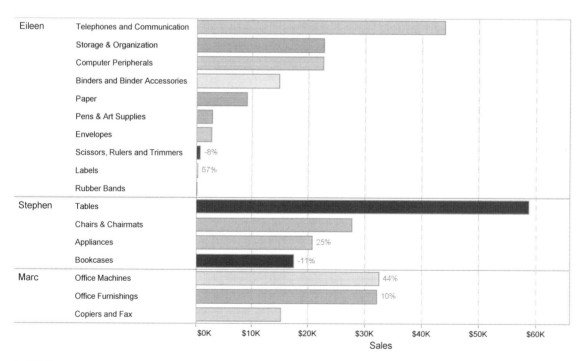

Profit Ratio
-11%  67%

Color and shape encode view elements for effective communication

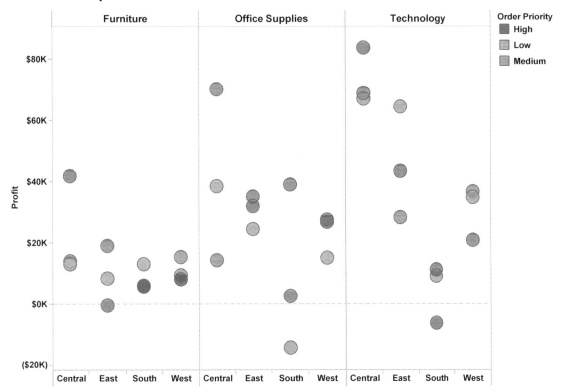

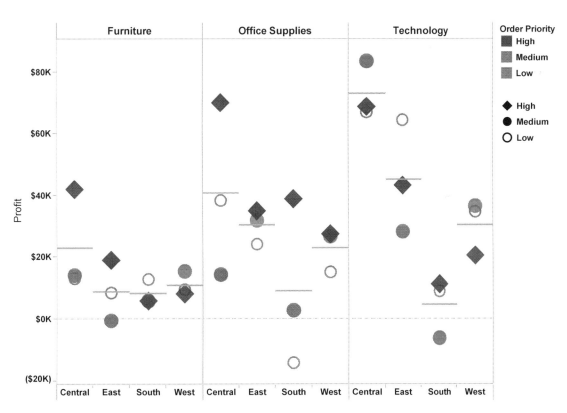

Simplicity

Getting started is easy if you follow the hands-on exercises in this book. In the first few weeks, you can learn the basics and begin mastering the techniques of graphical data exploration. Soon you will discover how to create visualizations that are more complex.

Areas of simplicity

- Direct interaction with graph—**drag and drop** what you want to see
- **Sort** the data **automatically or manually** directly from the view
- **Simple and complex grouping** of data items categories from the view
- **Exclude irrelevant data or keep only** the items of interest from the view
- **Automated calculations** such as *running total*, *change over prior year* or *year over year growth* without complex formulas
- Array of advanced **SQL calculations** for almost any need with any data source
- **Table calculations** allow advanced access to manipulate and calculate data items using the data returned from your data source
- Quickly add overall **subtotals**, specific-level subtotals and **grand totals**
- Readily explore the **data summarizing or underlying part of the view** with one click
- Shift from other views to **maps** of the data with one click
- Easily **export** your work to other applications such as **PowerPoint and Word**
- **Free Tableau Reader** allows interactive functionality for those outside your team
- **Publish your work to the web** for wide consumption of results in your company; no installation of any kind is required for web users to have a valuable subset of the desktop application functionality

Beauty

Create your own works of art while telling the story of your data! Keep your audience engaged and informed during presentations. Impress others with effective, clear communications that lead to lively discussions and actionable results. The interactive version of our dashboard shown on the facing page is available at http://www.Freakalytics.com/p/4 and is included as a sample with the standard installs of both Tableau Desktop and Tableau Server.

Tracking Economic Indicators and Stock Market Returns from 1901-2008
Relationships of Past, Present, and Future Values by Year

Select market metric to update bar chart
Real past 12 months return

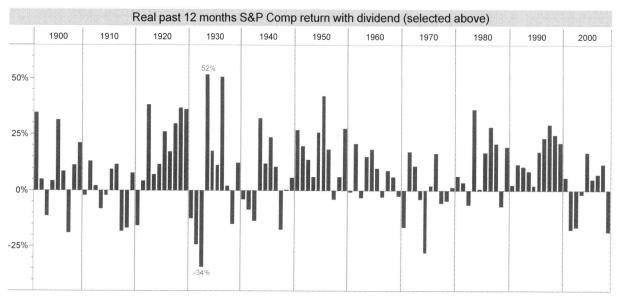

Select a range of years (Click+drag), a decade, or specific years (<CTRL>-Click) to highlight data below.

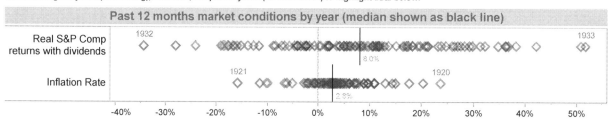

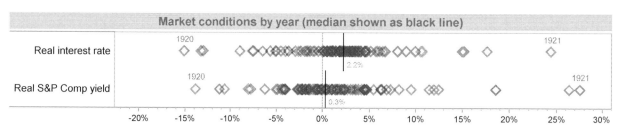

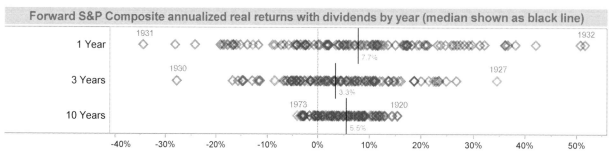

Chapter 2

Build the core—Tableau basics

Chapter Highlights

- Obtain and set up Tableau

- Sample data and the Tableau interface

- Your first view of Tableau

- Categorical data never looked so good!

To train for a marathon, you must first walk a mile. The good news is that learning Tableau is much easier than training for a marathon! In this chapter, you will walk through the first "few miles" of Tableau capabilities and even jog through the park a bit.

The first step in learning Tableau is to become acquainted with the application interface. Tableau's simplicity and elegance leads you forward in your analysis with ease while being flexible and responsive—once you learn the basics.

In the next two chapters, you will learn how to perform a broad range of analysis techniques. These chapters display a wide array of possibilities based upon only the core features of the application. At the conclusion of the next chapter, you will be familiar with the functionality and be able to start using Tableau in your work.

In this chapter, you will use a sample data source provided by Tableau, the **Sample—Coffee Chain (Access)** database.

Download, install and open Tableau

If you already have Tableau 8 installed on your PC, you can skip this section and go to the "Connect to sample data and review the Tableau interface" section.

Tableau offers a free software trial if you do not already own a license. The program requires a PC running Microsoft Windows (Version 7 or Version 8), Vista or XP, and you must have administrative rights on your computer to install it. It is important to note that Tableau has been tested and is supported on 64-bit Windows versions. Tableau is a 32-bit application and requires 32-bit versions of the database drivers, even when running on 64-bit versions of Windows.

Tableau can also be installed on Windows Server 2003, 2008, or 2012, which is primarily for corporate use on a shared server.

To download a free trial copy of Tableau Desktop, **go to** http://www.Freakalytics.com/RapidGraphs

Before you begin the download, **close all other applications and pause or disable your anti-virus and spyware prevention software. Additionally, you may need to obtain administrative rights to install software on your computer, or contact someone who already has them.** Note that these directions may vary depending on your operating system, anti-virus software, and other issues.

Once you click on the "Download Now" link on the Download Desktop page, you will be prompted to save the Tableau Desktop software. Click "Save File".

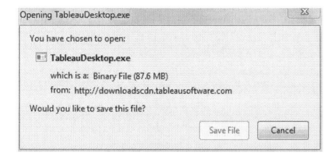

The file should automatically save to your download list, although you may need to choose a directory location.

Whether the installation file saved automatically or you chose a location, double click on it and then select "Run" on the dialog that appears.

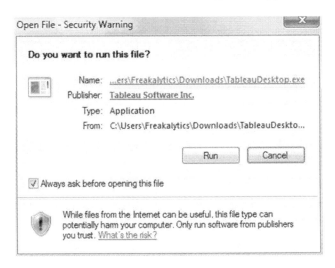

The Tableau Setup dialog appears. If you agree with the license terms, **check the box** to accept them and then **click "Install"**.

The Tableau Setup Welcome dialog

Then, the Activate Tableau dialog appears. **Select "Start trial now", fill out the registration form that appears and click Register.**

The Activate Tableau dialog

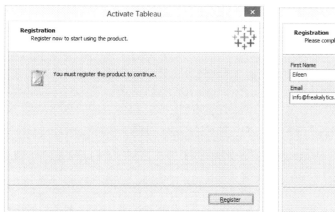 

After a few minutes, the installation should be complete and Tableau will automatically start. If you switched accounts to install Tableau, log out as administrator and log back in with your regular user account.

You are now ready to begin using Tableau. *Please note that if you are using the free trial, it will last 14 days from the first date you run the application.*

Connect to sample data and review the Tableau interface

Open Tableau from the Start menu of Windows, **Start → All Programs → Tableau 8**. By default, each time you open Tableau you will see the Start page.

The Tableau Start page

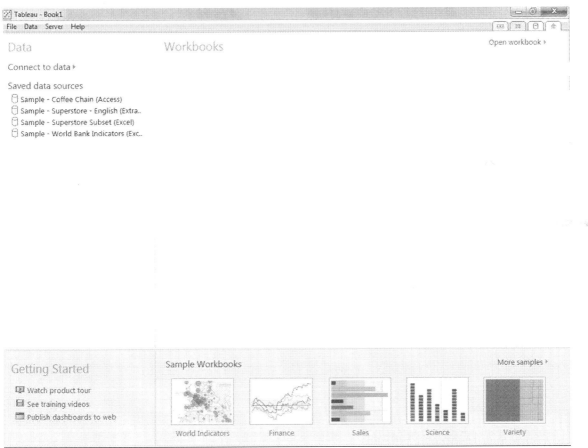

The Start page in Tableau has four sections, in addition to the Windows-type menu at the top left.

1. **Data** organizes your data sources. Click on **Connect to Data** to access new data sources or look under **Saved Data Sources** to select a data source that you've already saved, which at this point contains only sample datasets provided by Tableau.

2. The **Workbooks** section usually contains snapshots of your recent workbooks, but currently it's empty. Click on **Open workbook** to browse through your Tableau workbooks.

3. **Getting Started** lists support links.

4. The **Samples** section has many example workbooks provided by Tableau—browse through them for templates, ideas, and inspiration. In his role as Director of Analytics at Tableau Headquarters, Stephen collaborated with many experts to create and update these workbooks for Tableau 8. They include analyses in the areas of global economic data, finance, sales, science, education, government and much more.

In this chapter, you will use a sample data source provided by Tableau, the **Sample Coffee Chain** database. The Sample Coffee Chain is a fictitious national coffee chain. The dataset includes detailed sales, profit, and financial planning data for a 24-month period from January 2012 through December 2013. In the remainder of this chapter, you will answer a number of questions of interest for the management of this company.

Click on the Sample—Coffee Chain (Access) data source in the Data section on the Start page. The Tableau Workspace opens with the selected data source available for analysis. By default, the workbook is named Book 1.

! *Alternate Route:* All examples in this book use relational data sources, similar to Excel worksheets, Access tables or Oracle database tables. It is important to note that Tableau behaves differently in various parts of the application when using multi-dimensional data sources or "Cubes" (also called Microsoft Analysis Services, Essbase and other vendor names) as your data source. Although the vast majority of functionality is consistent across all databases, Tableau has specific features that are designed to leverage the benefits of each type of database while working within its constraints. You may be using one of these less common data sources and encounter different dialogs than those shown.

The Tableau Workspace with key areas numbered

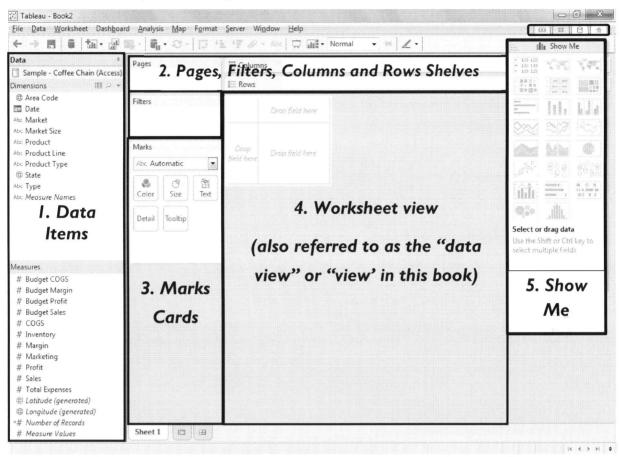

The Tableau Workspace has two standard features common to all Windows applications, the **file menu** across the top left of the workspace and a **toolbar** below it. Both behave as they normally do in Windows. You'll learn about the functions found on the various dropdowns of the file menu as you progress throughout the book, and the toolbar is shown in detail in the next chapter.

Specific to Tableau, there are **five key sections** of the interface which are labeled by number in the screenshot:

1. **Data Items pane (on the left):** shows information about the data source in use, including the name and list of data items. The data items are divided into **Dimensions** and **Measures**. Dimensions can be thought of as data "organizers" or "categories". Examples include location, date, product, and customer identifiers. Measures are measurements or calculations using your data. Examples include sales amount, profit, inventory on hand, cost of goods, and number of (data) records. In examples throughout the book, dimensions and measures are emphasized with gray, italicized text, e.g., *Dimension* or *Measure*.

   To the right of the word Dimensions, the small spreadsheet icon is the **View Data** button, and clicking on this displays the spreadsheet containing the data. The magnifying glass icon is the **Find Field** button, which offers a search box for data items or fields. There's also a dropdown menu with advanced selections which will become more useful as you learn Tableau.

2. **Pages, Filters, Columns and Rows Shelves (to the top right of the Data Items pane, under the toolbar):** where data items of interest are placed to control the data summarized and displayed in the Worksheet view (described in #4). We cover the functions of these shelves in detail throughout the book.

3. **Marks Card/s (to the right of the Data Items pane, under the Pages and Filters shelves):** in Tableau, data are displayed by **marks**, where every mark, or data point, represents a row or group of rows found in the original data source. These cards allow you to control how the data items are presented in the Worksheet view. For example, for selected marks, you can specify whether or not to display text or labels, as well as change shapes, colors, and sizes, such as the width of the mark.

4. **Worksheet view, data view, or view (large space):** where the summarized data are displayed in tables or graphs. This is where all of your requests come together for your review and analysis or for presentation to colleagues.

5. **Show Me dialog (rectangular box on the right):** Show Me is a "smart" chart selector where most of your analyses will begin, especially when you're learning how to use Tableau, but it's an invaluable timesaver for advanced users as well.

Workspace Controls

The **workspace controls** are the four small tabs at the top right of the workspace under the minimize, maximize and close tabs (unmarked in the screenshot). You can use them to toggle between various screens in Tableau. The first tab, with three squares sandwiched in between two lines, brings up the Tableau Workspace. The second tab, with four squares, is a "worksheet sorter" that shows thumbnail pictures of the various worksheets you are working on, so you can select the one you want. The third tab, the cylinder that represents a data source, takes you to a detailed **Connect to Data** page to help you find particular data sources. The fourth tab, the house, brings you back "home" to the Tableau Start Page.

"Show Me" Tableau in action

The CFO of the Sample Coffee Chain is interested in a simple two-year view of sales, profit, and profit versus planned profit by month. She would like this information on one page for her monthly team reviews so she can hand it out without wasting too much paper. Additionally, she wants to easily contrast the current year with the prior year. In this first example, you will create this view.

1. **While holding down the <Ctrl> key on your keyboard, move your mouse to the Data Items pane and click on** *Date* **in the Dimensions section and** *Sales* **in the Measures section**. The <Ctrl> key allows you to select multiple data items at one time. The Show Me dialog automatically changes—now the *lines (discrete)* graph type is selected by Tableau, shown by the blue outline, and described in the text at the bottom of the dialog. Note that if you hover over the icons of the different data views this text will change to match the highlighted view type. **Click on the** *lines (discrete)* **icon** to accept it. To hide the Show Me dialog so it is not in your way, **click anywhere on the light blue bar at the top of it**.

The Show Me dialog defaults to the *lines (discrete)* **graph type**

The initial view—*Sales* by *Year*

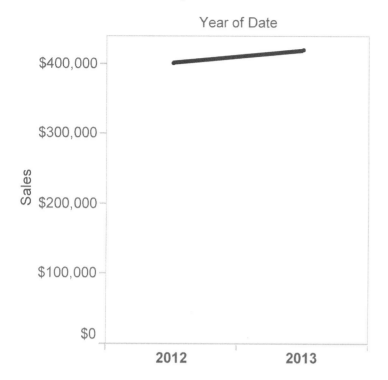

Year of Date

Note that even though *Date* is at the month level in the dataset, the data view automatically started at the year level. Dates in Tableau default to a hierarchical arrangement — Year, Quarter, Month and Day.

In addition, *Sales* became *SUM(Sales)* on the Rows shelf. In this case, the sales values displayed in the view are *sums* of individual sales values. This will make more sense as you progress through the book, but how the data item is displayed on the shelves lets you know how Tableau *aggregates* the data shown in the view.

2. In data analysis software, to "drill down" means to move from a summarized data item to a more detailed view of the item (if more levels of detail exist). Drill down from an annual view to a quarterly and monthly view of the data. You can drill down on dates by **clicking the + (plus) sign immediately before the *YEAR(Date)* variable in the Columns shelf** (near the center of the Workspace under the toolbar). **Click on the + sign for** *Year*. *Quarter* will appear to the right on the Columns shelf and visually in the Worksheet. **Click on the + sign for** *Quarter*. *Month* also will appear both on the shelf and in the Worksheet view.

Use the plus sign on drillable data items to drill down

The view after drill-down—*Sales* by *Year*, *Quarter*, and *Month*

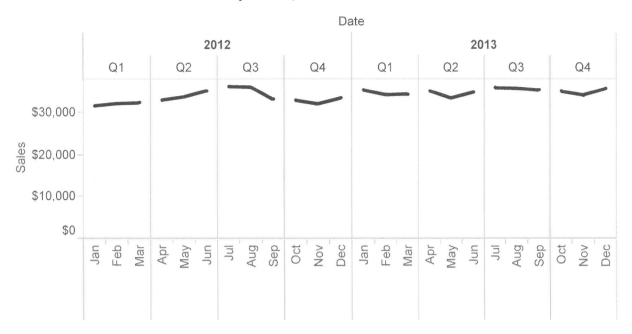

3. Since *Quarter* makes this view busy, remove it. **Click on QUARTER(Date) in the Columns shelf and without releasing the click, drag QUARTER(Date) to any spot on the screen except for the graph, shelves or Marks Card, and then release it** (this is called "drag and drop"). Notice how the view dynamically updates with each action.

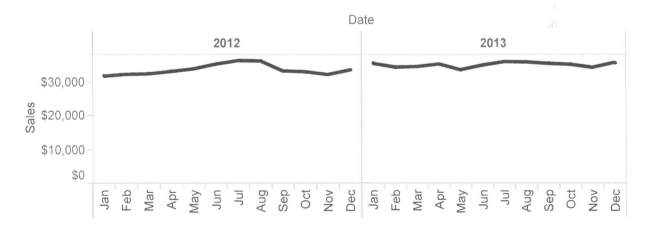

! Performance Tip: When you drag and drop to remove an item off a shelf, you do not need to drop the item in any specific place—as soon as a little red X appears, when you drop the data item, it will be removed from the view.

4. Since we intend to contrast year over year changes, you can color code the different years by using the *Year* level of the *Date* data item. **Drag and drop *Year* from the Columns shelf on top of the Color button on the Marks Card.** To ensure that you target the right button, the Color button should turn light orange before you drop the item on it. 2012 becomes a continuous blue line and 2013 a continuous orange line (shown here in greyscale). Looks good!

**The view with Year contrasted by color coding
(in your view, blue = 2012 and orange = 2013)**

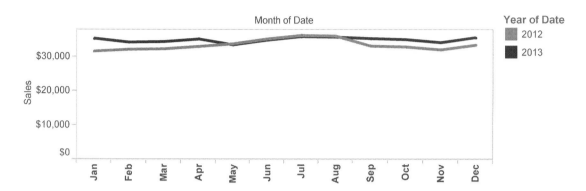

5. **Drag the *Profit* data item from the Measures pane to the Rows shelf and drop it after the SUM(Sales) data item.** This demonstrates how any view can be built using drag and drop instead of the Show Me dialog.

Sales **contrasted with** *Profit*

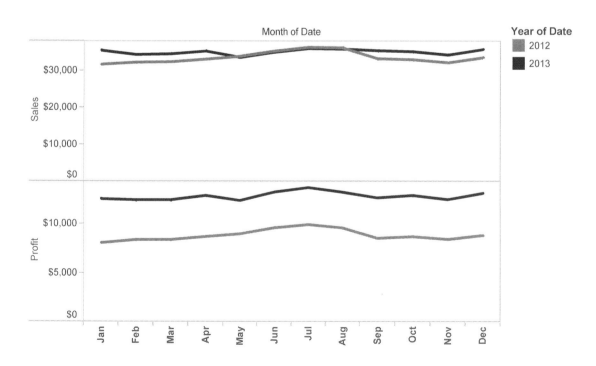

6. Finally, notice there is no data item that compares profit and planned profit. There are *Profit* and *Budget Profit* data items. You can use these two data items to create a calculated data item, *Profit vs. Plan*. **Right-click on** *Profit* **in the Data Items pane and a context menu appears. Select Create Calculated Field from the menu**. The Calculated Field dialog appears.

7. In the Formula pane of the Calculated Field, the data item *Profit* is preselected for the formula. After [Profit], **add a minus sign (—) and then double-click on** *Budget Profit* in the Fields section of the dialog. The formula should now read, "[Profit] — [Budget Profit]". Tableau automatically checks the formula for validity—since this formula is valid, a green check appears next to the statement "The calculation is valid." In the **Name section at the top of the dialog, change the name to "Profit vs. Plan". Click OK**. The new calculated field appears in the Measures section of the Data Items pane, with an equals sign, =, to the left of the name, to signify that it is a calculated data item.

The Calculated Field dialog with the formula for Profit vs. Plan

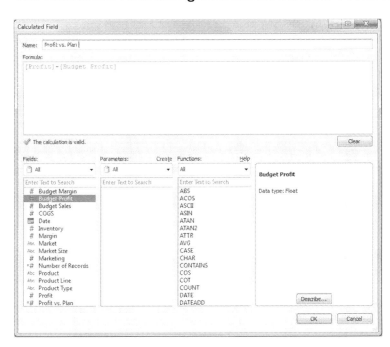

8. **Add the calculated data item** *Profit vs. Plan* **to the Rows shelf after the** *SUM(Profit)* **data item by drag and drop**. The worksheet is now complete! Note the **status bar** at the far bottom left of the workspace, which describes what you have in the current view. There are 72 marks in 3 rows (*Sales*, *Profit*, and *Profit vs. Plan*) by 12 columns (12 months) and *Sum of Profit vs. Plan* across the 24 marks (2 years, one year below and one year above overall) is $783. Depending on your computer's settings, you may have to use the scrollbar on the right to see the entire view. **To display the entire view at once and eliminate the scrollbar, click the dropdown next to the word** *Normal* **on the toolbar and select** *Entire View*.

The analysis requested by Sample Coffee Chain's CFO

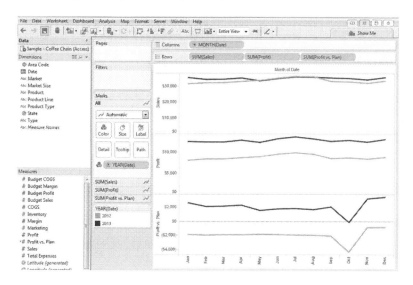

A very informative view:

- The "Sales" graph shows that sales are barely higher in 2013 than in 2012, with the summer being flat year over year.

- However, if you look at the "Profit" graph, 2013 has much higher profit levels than 2012. Apparently, in 2013, the company either controlled expenses better or increased prices or sales volume enough to boost profits 40-50%.

- Finally, the "Profit vs. Plan" graph suggests that the company has some quirks in budget planning because the projected profits were inaccurate. There is usually a difference between actual and planned profits (except in October 2013). The good news is that the company is significantly above planned 2013 profits, a welcome improvement from 2012 where it was always below planned profits. Unfortunately, a spike in profitability was planned for both years, something that should be adjusted or removed in the plan for 2014.

To make it easy for the CFO to use this analysis, you have four options. The CFO could use Tableau or the free Tableau Reader downloadable from the Tableau website. You could export the view to a PDF by **selecting the File → Print to PDF menu item.** You could also copy the view as an image, by **right-clicking on the Worksheet view and selecting Copy → Image.** If you want the view in PowerPoint, the Copy Image feature is the best route. When you select this option, you will be prompted for details about what parts of the view to export and details about legend usage in the copied image.

Categorically clear views

The regional sales managers of Sample Coffee Chain are interested in an analysis of profit by product. They will use these data to discuss growth opportunities for new products and possible pricing changes or product cancellation ideas. Here you will create a simple view to show profitability by product.

1. **Click on the Worksheet menu and select New Worksheet**. A new worksheet is added to the project, named Sheet 2 by default.

2. **While holding down the <Ctrl> key on your keyboard, move your mouse to the Data Items pane and click on** *Product* **in the Dimensions section and** *Profit* **in the Measures section. Click the blue bar at the top of the Show Me dialog to unhide it.** The *horizontal bars* graph type is automatically selected by Tableau. **Click on the icon.** A horizontal bar chart with profit by product is generated in the Worksheet view. **Hide the Show Me dialog.** An alternative to clicking on the top of Show Me to hide and unhide the dialog is **<Ctrl> + 1.**

Horizontal bar chart of *Profit* by *Product*

Much easier to read than the typical vertical bar chart!

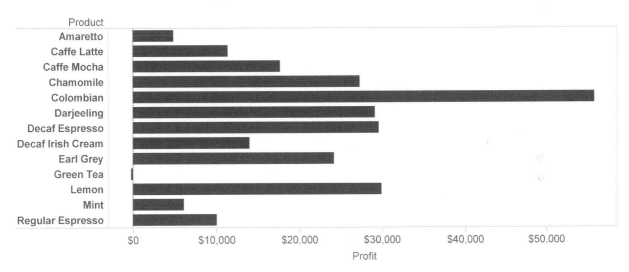

3. To highlight the highest profit products, sort the bars by profit. If you hover with your mouse over the *Product* oval on the Rows Shelf, a down caret appears. **Click on the down caret and select Sort from the drop down context menu.** The Sort dialog opens.

The down caret for accessing the context menu

The context menu available from dimensions placed on the shelf

4. The Sort dialog has the default settings of Sort Order: Ascending for Sort by Data Source Order. **Change the Sort Order to Descending and the Sort by to Field.** *Profit* **is already selected in the drop down. Click OK**. The bar graph is now sorted in descending profit order by each product.

The Sort dialog for Product

Product is now sorted in descending order by _Profit_

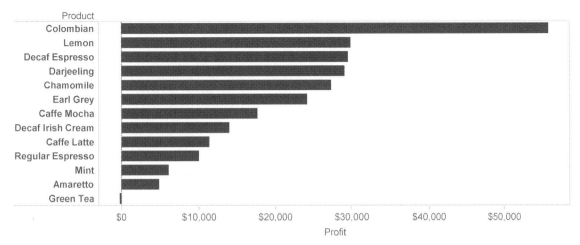

! Alternate Route: You will learn more about sorting your data in a later chapter, but a quick shortcut to sorting measures that are currently in use is to click on the Sort Ascending and Sort Descending buttons on the toolbar, which look like this:

If you hover over these buttons, they will tell you what will be sorted; in this case, "Sort Product ascending by Profit". Also, a descending sort icon appears directly in the view, to the right of the label of the data item sorted; in this case, Profit.

5. Since the regional managers will be interested in the performance of their respective markets, you should add _Market_ to the view. **Drag and drop _Market_ from the Dimensions pane to the Columns shelf just to the left of** _SUM(Profit)_. Tableau indicates where the item will drop by displaying a tiny blue inverted caret behind the _Market_ field. Note that the sorting is based on the overall profit across all four regions, not any particular region!

Profit by Product and Market/Region, sorted based on overall profit across all four regions

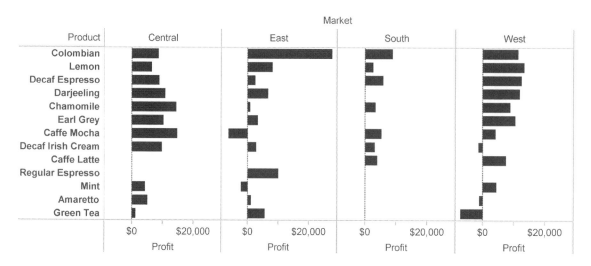

6. To highlight profitability levels, **add** *Profit* **directly from the Measures section of the Data Items pane to the Color button of the Marks Card** (do not drag it from the Columns Shelf because your bar chart with be converted to a table). Tableau automatically uses a red-green contrast to show negative profitability as red and positive profitability as green. Tableau also uses the intensity of the two colors to show lower or higher values. The result is that lower and higher values stand in great contrast. Profit is now "color-encoded".

Profit by Product and Market/Region with Profit color-encoded
Low profit items stand out
(in your view, dark red is low profit and dark green is high profit)

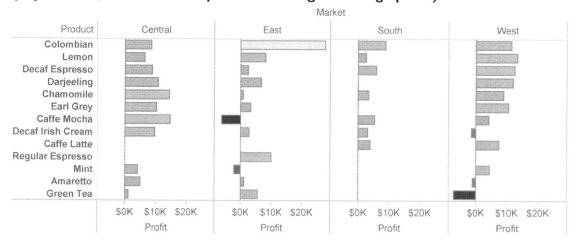

Profit

($7K) $27K

A few products have negative profits, and one product, Colombian, has relatively high profit, but only in the East.

7. Finally, since the regional managers are interested in understanding profitability of various products in their own regions, the shape of the distribution in each region is informative. However, it is likely even more informative to color encode the value by the profit results versus the planned profit results. Why? This is because pricing may not result in the high profits that are expected for certain products. To enable this view, one simple change is required—**replace** *Profit* **by dragging and dropping** *Profit vs. Plan* **on top of the Color button**.

Profit by Product and Market with Profit vs. Plan color-encoded

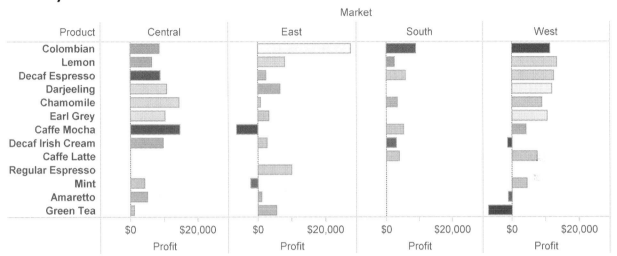

This final view reveals a great amount of information. The overall shape of profitability varies across the four regions with no clear pattern. Additionally, some of the highest profit items in the regions are often the worst performing products relative to plan (for instance, Caffe Mocha in the Central Region). This information would likely lead to different plans for future product directions depending on the region, suggesting that product line strategy should be managed at the regional level.

Chapter 3

Go with the flow—more Tableau basics

Chapter Highlights

- Get mileage out of the Tableau toolbar!

- Table the data for an in-depth view

- Maps and geographical results

- View shifting with histograms and bins

- Sharing the insights created in Tableau

Great—already, you have learned enough about the features and workflow of Tableau to begin analyzing data! Now, you're ready to explore more possibilities. The regional sales managers and product planners have seen your initial results. They are excited and ready to pepper you with more questions.

In this chapter, first you'll learn about the many useful shortcuts found on the toolbar. Then, you'll return to the task at hand, answering colleagues' questions by creating advanced tables and insightful maps, and transforming histograms into advanced bar charts to get your point across to your audience. The chapter concludes with a brief overview of the many ways that you can deliver your findings to your team, customers, and anyone else.

In this chapter, you will use a sample data source provided by Tableau, the **Sample—Coffee Chain (Access)** database.

Save time with the Tableau toolbar

Tableau has only one toolbar. You can perform many common tasks quickly by clicking the buttons on the toolbar.

The Tableau Toolbar

We have included useful information about the toolbar buttons in the following table.

Button	Name	Action	Shortcut Keys/ Alternative Routes
← →	Undo and Redo	Undo or redo last action Both can be used repeatedly until you close	**Undo:** <Ctrl> + Z **Redo:** <Ctrl> + Y
▪	Save	Save workbook	<Ctrl> + S
▪	Connect to Data	Connect to data sources such as Excel or Access	<Ctrl> + D
🔳 🔳 🔳	New sheet, Duplicate sheet, Clear sheet	Whole worksheet actions	**New:** <Ctrl> + M **Dup:** Right-click on worksheet tab **Clear:** <Ctrl> + <Alt> + Backspace
🔳 🔁	Automatic Update, Run Update	Data source query	**Automatic:** F10 toggles on/off **Run:** F9; use to update when automatic is turned off
🔳	Swap	Exchanges rows and columns	<Ctrl> + W
🔳 🔳	Sort Ascending, Sort Descending	Sort a particular data item	Right-click on the header of a dimension and sort options will appear
🖉	Group Members	Creates new data item from two or more individual dimensions	Right-click on a dimension and select **Create Group**

Button	Name	Action	Shortcut Keys/ Alternative Routes
Abc	**Show Mark Labels**	Labels data points with names or values	On the **Marks Card → Label button** dropdown, check the **Show Mark Labels** box
	Presentation Mode	Hides everything except for the view, legends and quick filters	<Ctrl> + H
	Show/Hide Cards	View Cards dropdown menu, for changing cards and shelves	**Main menu→ Worksheet** has some of the options
Normal ▾	**Fit selector**	Dropdown sizes the view—options are Normal, Fit Width, Fit Height, Entire View	Manually resize by dragging borders of the view
	Fix Axes	Toggle button that clears specific axes to a selected range or displays the entire range	Right-click on axis and select **Edit Axis** menu
	Highlight	Menu with options for turning highlighting on/off	<Ctrl> + Select marks to highlight directly within the view

! Performance Tip: Check out the table of useful keyboard shortcuts in the appendix of this book. These can save you even more time in your daily work.

When tables trump graphs

After the regional sales managers reviewed your analysis of profit by product, the West sales manager called and asked for more details. He said that his area managers could not agree on the weak and strong products so they were interested in examining product profit by small versus major markets. To examine the details, you'll use a "heat map" color-coded data table. Heat map color-coding uses color to represent or highlight the values or intensities of data items so that minimum and maximum values stand out.

1. **On the Start menu, open the Sample—Coffee Chain (Access) data source, or, if you still have it open from the last exercise, click on the Worksheet menu and select New Worksheet**. A new worksheet is added to the project.

2. **While holding down the <Ctrl> key on your keyboard, move your mouse to the Data Items pane and click on** *Date*, *Market Size* **and** *Product* **in the Dimensions area and** *Profit* **in the Measures area. Open Show Me**, and the dialog will appear with the *lines(discrete)* graph type automatically selected by Tableau. **Change and select the data view by clicking on** *text tables* **in the upper left corner**. A *text table* will appear in the Worksheet view, which also is called a crosstab. **Hide Show Me**.

   Where are the missing products? **Click on the scroll bar along the bottom of the table.**

Profit for Market Size by Product and Year

	Amaretto		Caffe Latte		Caffe Mocha		Chamomile	
Market Size	2012	2013	2012	2013	2012	2013	2012	2013
Major Market	$811	$1,203	$2,384	$3,470	$4,005	$5,813	$4,644	$6,756
Small Market	$1,172	$1,704	$2,252	$3,269	$3,196	$4,664	$6,449	$9,382

Product / Year of Date

3. Since we are examining the West region only, **drag** *Market* **from the Dimensions area of the Data Items pane and drop it on the Filters shelf**. The Filter dialog will appear. **Click on "West" and click OK**.

The Filter Dialog

! Performance Tip: If you are working with a large or slow database, filter the data before you add any items to the view (after Step 1 in this section).

4. Now you have only data from the West in your text table. Since you are particularly interested in the products with negative profit, color encode the profit data by **dragging** *Profit* **from the Measures area of the Data Items to the Color button on the Marks Card.**

   a. By default, a measure with negative and positive values will encode the negative values as red and the positive values as green.

   b. The color encoding is coloring only the text of the profit values, not the background of the cells. To amplify the highlighting of the profit values, add some color encoding of the cells. **Unhide Show Me and click on *highlight tables* in the second row, center, to change the graph type, then hide Show Me.**

Profit for *Market Size* by *Product* and *Year* with Color Highlighting (West Markets only)

Product / Year of Date

Market Size	Amaretto		Caffe Latte		Caffe Mocha		Chamomile	
	2012	2013	2012	2013	2012	2013	2012	2013
Major Market	($912)	($1,305)	$1,834	$2,663	$362	$524	$1,328	$1,924
Small Market	$402	$591	$1,224	$1,781	$1,294	$1,886	$2,280	$3,322

Profit

($1,324) $1,290

5. Drill down on the *Date* data item by **clicking on the + sign to the left of the word** *Year*. *Quarter(Date)* appears next to the *Year(Date)* data item.

! *Alternate Route*: **To drill down, you can hover over the** *Date* **data labels directly in the view and click on the + sign that appears to the left of the axis. In this case, hover over 2013 and 2012 and the + sign will appear.**

6. To enable easier comparison of year over year changes in profit by quarter, move quarters to the rows side of the text table by **dragging the** *Quarter* **data item from the Columns shelf and dropping it on the Rows shelf next to** *Market Size*.

7. To summarize the profit across both market sizes for each year, turn on the column totals. **On the main menu, select Analysis → Totals → Show Column Grand Totals.**

8. To emphasize not only profit level, but growth or reduction in profit from year to year, change the color coding to year over year growth rate in profit. **On the Marks Card, find the shaded oval labeled "SUM(Profit)" that has the Color button** <u>icon</u> **to the left of it (three colored bubbles). Hover over it and click on the down caret that appears.** A context menu opens. **Scroll to Quick Table Calculation** near the bottom of the menu and a submenu appears—**click on Year over Year Growth**.

Context Menu and Submenu for Profit Color Coding

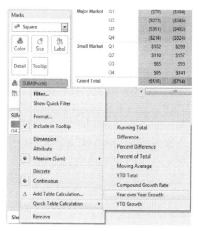

Profit by Market Size for West Markets by Year and Quarter,
Color Highlighting by Year over Year Growth

Product / Year of Date

% Difference in Profit

-48.6% ——— 51.5%

Market Size	Quarter of Date	Amaretto		Caffe Latte		Caffe Mocha		Chamomile	
		2012	2013	2012	2013	2012	2013	2012	2013
Major Market	Q1	($70)	($104)	$431	$650	$70	$105	$303	$457
	Q2	($273)	($385)	$478	$676	$87	$124	$350	$494
	Q3	($351)	($492)	$490	$692	$121	$170	$387	$545
	Q4	($218)	($324)	$435	$645	$84	$125	$288	$428
Small Market	Q1	$132	$200	$354	$534	$268	$404	$587	$887
	Q2	$110	$157	$339	$480	$278	$393	$561	$794
	Q3	$65	$93	$288	$406	$326	$463	$552	$780
	Q4	$95	$141	$243	$361	$422	$626	$580	$861
Grand Total		($510)	($714)	$3,058	$4,444	$1,656	$2,410	$3,608	$5,246

- Since the light red cells in your view (shown as dark cells here) are negative profit growth quarters (year over year), a quick review of this table highlights the fact that unprofitable market sizes in 2012 have become even more unprofitable in 2013, a troubling trend.

- Likewise, market sizes that were profitable in 2012 are even more profitable in 2013, a good trend.

- The table highlights that unprofitable products overall are always profitable in at least one of the two overall market sizes. This is a bit surprising and perhaps shows a need for further research and possible changes in market-based offerings.

! Performance Tip: The Marks card, which you used in this example, is a very powerful tool that quickly alters the appearance of the items in your view. It's covered in detail in a later chapter.

Insightful maps

After the regional sales managers reviewed your analysis of profit by product, they scheduled a follow-up meeting and asked for a map to distribute to the state managers. The CEO's request: "Everyone loves maps. We want to distribute the state-by-state results on a map that is simple to understand. Show us how well each manager adjusted their profitability plans after an abysmal job planning profitability in 2012!"

To meet this specific request, you will use a "Map" view with color-coded values for profit versus plan.

1. On the keyboard, **select <Ctrl> and M at the same time to add a New Worksheet (abbreviated <Ctrl> + M from now on).**

2. **While holding down the <Ctrl> key on your keyboard, move your mouse to Data Items and click on** *Date* **and** *State* **in the Dimensions area and** *Profit* **in the Measures area. Unhide Show Me.** The *symbol map* graph type is automatically selected by Tableau—**click on it.** Two side-by-side maps will appear displaying *Profit* (shown by the size of the bubbles or "size-encoded") by *State* and *Year.* **Hide Show Me.**

   Any time your mouse pointer hovers over a map, you will see a navigation tool appear in the upper left area of the map. For details on using this tool, see the Zoom Controls section of the Appendix at the back of this book.

! *Performance Tip:* Note that if you are offline, a dialog box will pop up saying that you cannot load the online map. **Click OK and select Map → Background Maps → Offline.**

Profit *by* State *and* Year, Profit *is Size-Encoded (bubble size)*

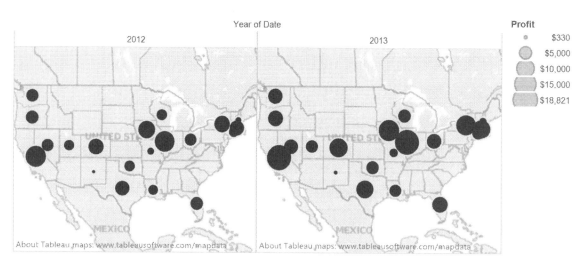

! *Alternate Route:* After Step 1 in this section, **double-click on** *State, Date* **and** *Profit,* **in that order.**

3. The maps would be easier to look at if they were stacked rather than side-by-side. **Drag** *Year(Date)* **from the Columns shelf and drop it on the Rows Shelf to the left of the** *Latitude (Generated)* **data item**. The map view updates with the 2012 map placed above the 2013 map.

4. You should now have the states with the biggest profits already displayed. It will be useful to highlight their performance by comparing them with planned profits. To add *Profit vs. Plan* to the view (the calculated field created in the last chapter), **drag and drop** *Profit vs. Plan* **from Data Items to the Color button on the Marks Card.**

5. The bubbles for each state are now color-encoded based on the size of the difference in dollars of profit versus planned profit (or how off the plans were!). The sizes of the bubbles did not change (they still represent profit only). In the view on your screen, deep red is very bad (the planned profits were way above the actual profits!), red is bad, gray is neutral (expected), light green is good (exceeded plan), and dark green is very good. Note that it's not only easy to see the most profitable states quickly, but the states with the worst and best performance relative to plan also stand out.

**Profit by State by Year, Profit versus Plan Color-Encoded in your view
(In this illustration, dark = negative values and light = positive values)**

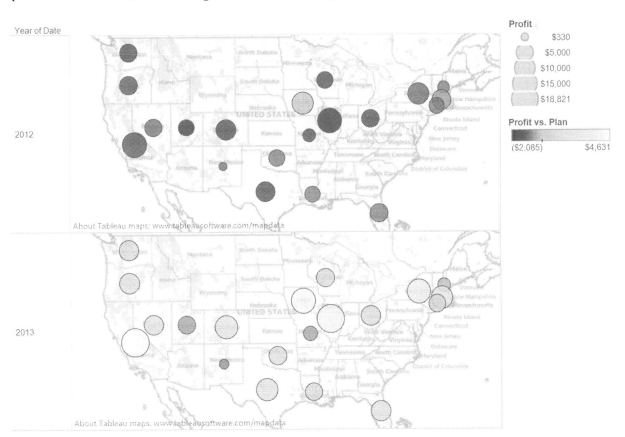

6. Since managers are often very interested in the details of just how far off their plans were from the outcome, you can give them this information in the map as a ratio of profit vs. planned profit. Create a new calculated data item, *Profit as a % of Plan*. **Right-click on** *Profit* **in the Data Items pane.** A context menu appears. **Select Create Calculated Field from the menu**. The Calculated Field dialog appears.

7. In the Formula pane of the Calculated Field, the data item *Profit* is preselected for the formula. **Edit the formula so that it reads:**
   Sum([Profit]) / Sum([Budget Profit])

8. In the **Name section of the dialog, change the name to "Profit as a % of Plan". Click OK**. The new calculated field appears in the Measures part of the Data Items pane.

9. **Drag the calculated data item** *Profit as a % of Plan* **to the Label button on the Marks Card.** Labels appear on the map.

10. Since you want this metric to be displayed as a percentage, you should format it. **On the Marks Card, right-click on the shaded oval** *AGG(Profit as a % of Plan)* **that has the Label icon to the left of it** (it says "Abc123"). A context menu appears. **Select Format from the menu**. The Format pane replaces the Data Items pane on the left side of the Tableau application.

The Format Pane

11. Under the Default heading, click on the dropdown (the down caret) in the Numbers selector. A dialog appears. Select Percentage and change the Decimal places setting to "0". To close the Format Pane, click on the "x" in the upper right corner. The Data Items pane reappears to the left of the final map, which is shown below.

Size Encoding Profit by State and Year,
Color Encoding of Profit versus Plan, Text Showing Profit as a % of Plan
(In this illustration, dark = negative values and light = positive values)

This map communicates a lot of information and mostly good news! Managers can quickly compare themselves with their peer states and all other states for both years. To easily interpret the features that you added to the map, look at one at a time:

- First, compare bubble sizes between states to see which states are bigger markets. Also, compare bubble sizes in 2012 with those in 2013 to see which states had bigger increases in profitability. For example, California and Illinois had strong growth in profit, which is great, since they also are larger markets.

- Look at the color-coding on your screen. Notice that in 2012 virtually the entire map is red, so planned profits were more than the actual profits (not good!), while in 2013 almost every state was green (good!). The more intense the red, the more inaccurate the plan, but keep in mind that these represent dollar amounts, so a dark red small bubble may not be as detrimental to the company's overall planned profits as a light red large bubble. Fortunately, the dark red bubbles in 2012 were in smaller markets (smaller bubbles) except for Illinois, which was darker green by 2013.

- The percentages tell you how inaccurate the plans were. The lower the percentage, the worse the performance of the state relative to plan. In addition to quantifying how "off" the plans were, these are different than just looking at the color coding because they are relative measurements, so you can compare smaller markets with larger markets. In 2012, New Mexico was way off—profits totaled only 25% of the planned profits but Iowa almost reached the planned profits at 99%. 2013 was a completely new ball game—the vast majority of states met or exceeded their plans! In fact, the most profitable states vastly exceeded their plans by 20-40%.

View shifting—the underrated histogram and flexible bins

One of the product planners wants to provide the regional sales managers with a better understanding of the importance of lower volume items. She tells you that the higher volume products often get all the "love" and she wanted to see if her hunch was right, that the lower volume products are more important than commonly given credit.

After thinking about the best way to present this information, you realize an advanced form of a histogram (a bar chart that shows *counts* of items divided by category) would offer abundant insight into this question.

To meet this specific request, you will use a "Histogram" view with size- and color-coded values for profit. You will categorize sales into "bins" to create the histogram chart bars.

1. **Use <Ctrl> + M to add a New Worksheet.**

2. **Click on** *Sales* **in the Measures area and open Show Me**. The Show Me dialog will appear with the *horizontal bars* graph type automatically selected by Tableau. **Change the view type to *histogram*,** shown in Show Me as single bar chart with a central peak. **Click it and hide Show Me**. A *histogram of Sales* will appear with count of sales records automatically binned into dollar intervals of 100: 0 to 99 is the 0 bar, 100 to 199 is the 100 bar, and so on.

Sales histogram—display the volume of orders by sale amount

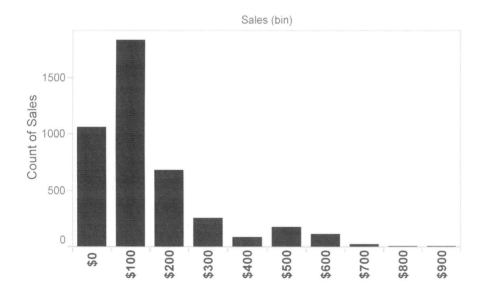

3. You want to know "what the dataset looks like" behind the view. To see the data in a more familiar spreadsheet form, **right-click on the view and select View Data (**we will cover this feature more in a later chapter).

4. Note that due to the data used in this sample, a count of sales records in each bin is not very useful. This is a simple summary of the number of monthly sales records for each item in each area code. To make this much more informative, change *CNT (Sales)* to *SUM (Sales)*. **Click on the down caret next to *CNT (Sales)* on the Rows Shelf, select Measure (Count) and change the aggregate function to Sum.** The ***histogram*** is now considered a ***horizontal bars*** chart by Tableau, so you will see this if you click on Show Me. Technically, this is no longer a histogram because it does not display counts, but you used the histogram as a basis to describe the sales data.

   ! *Alternate Route:* You could have first binned the data and then used a *horizontal bars* chart. Binning is covered in a later chapter.

5. Next, you want to differentiate between year and region. **From the Data pane, add *Date* to the Columns Shelf to the left of the *Sales (bin)* item already there and add *Market* to the Rows Shelf to the left of the *SUM(Sales)* data item.** Eight charts appear in the view—each of these is referred to as a pane.

Sales Histogram by Year and Market

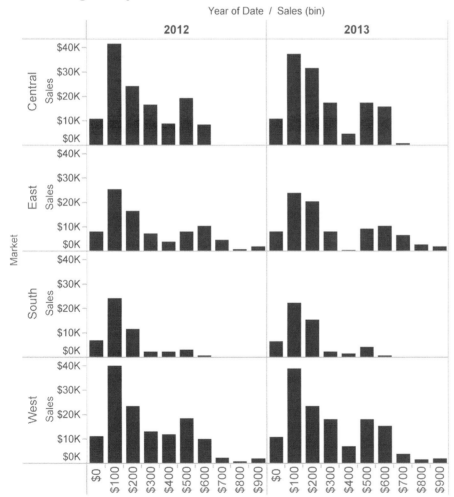

Note the different patterns found in the different regions. West and Central have pronounced peaks at $100 and $500, East and South have less pronounced peaks at $100 and East has more data at the upper end of the binned sales.

Next, add profitability to contrast with sales. Similar to what you did above on the map, you'll color-code the bars, size the bars, and place profit percentages above each bar.

6. **From the Measures area, add** *Profit* **three times to the Marks Card: Color, Size, and Label buttons.**

! Alternate Route: **Add** *Profit* **once to the Color button. Press <Ctrl> and simultaneously click and drag** *Profit* **from the Color button and drop it on both the Size and Label buttons.** This duplicates *Profit* without dragging it from the Measures pane two more times. This neat trick also works on other shelves.

7. Clean this up—the text is busy and detracts from the key purpose of the view. To better calculate the profit that is above each sales bin bar so that it is easier to understand, change it from sum of profit to percent of profit for that pane. **On the Marks Card, click on the down caret on the Label oval containing** *SUM (Profit)* **and select Add Table Calculation from the dropdown.** The Table Calculation dialog appears. **In the Table Calculation dialog, change Calculation Type to Percent of Total. This changes the option under Calculation Definition to "Summarize the values from:". Select Pane from the drop down, and click OK.**

The Table Calculation dialog alters the calculation type

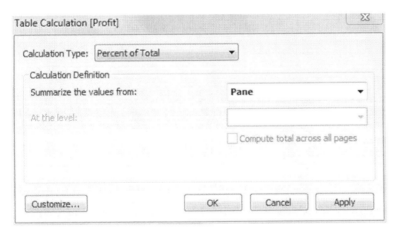

8. **The text values change to percentages in each view pane. These percentages are the percent of total profit for that pane in each binned sales bar. Notice that the default format is too precise for this purpose. Right-click on the Label oval containing** *SUM (Profit)* **on the Marks Card, and select Format from the context menu.** The Format pane replaces the Data Items pane on the left side of the Tableau application. **Click on the dropdown next to the Default Numbers selector, and when a dialog appears, select Percentage and change the Decimal places setting to "0". To close the Format Pane, click on the "x" at the upper right corner.** The Data Items pane reappears to the left of the view.

Sales Binned by Year and Market, Profit highlighted as percent of pane and encoded by both color and bar size

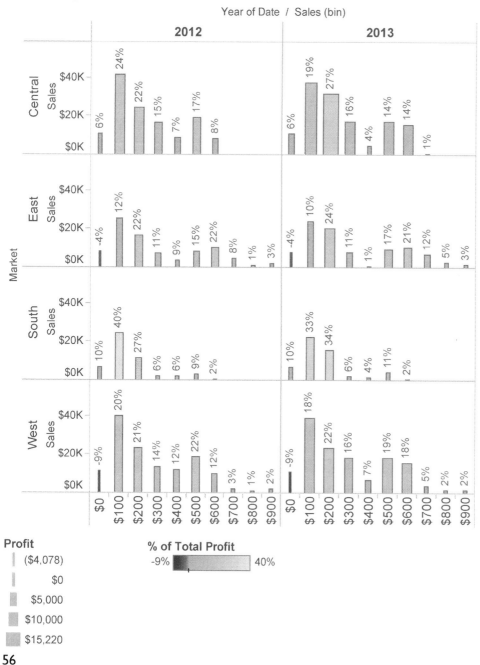

Profit

| ($4,078)
| $0
▮ $5,000
▮ $10,000
▮ $15,220

% of Total Profit

-9% ▮▮▮▮▮▮▮▮ 40%

56

You meet with the product planner to explain this insightful view. Some key insights stand out:

Examining the binned monthly sales amounts on the horizontal axis, you can see that the highest revenue products are a relatively minor portion of the profits (profit percentage contribution is at top of each bar) across the entire company. For example, the East saw just 4%-8% of all profits generated by products generating revenue of $800-$1,000 per month.

Examining the annual sales represented by bar heights, you can observe that although products with the highest total sales are typically quite profitable, they rarely generate the greatest profitability. For example, in the West in 2013, $100 per month products generated the greatest sales, but only 18% of profits, so they were not the highest profit makers in the pane. That would be products in the $200 bin (22%) followed by products in the $500 bin (19%). The South region is the exception: in 2012, the $100 bin generated the most profit (40%), and in 2013, the $100 bin (33%) was essentially tied for the highest profit with the $200 bin (34%).

The East and West have pronounced profitability at the mid-sales volume product areas, with more than 34% to 40% of all profits being generated by these products, generating sales of $500-$700 per month.

Another interesting point about this view is that the data in each pane exhibit a primary peak in annual sales at around $100 and a secondary peak at around $500. This is called a bimodal distribution.

Exporting results to share your insights

You have several options for distributing your results:

1) Sit down with the recipients and interactively explore the results and data via Tableau.

2) Install a copy of Tableau or a free Tableau Reader (downloadable from the Tableau website) for the recipients and share your Tableau project. Tableau has a server product built to make this sharing centralized and more manageable.

3) Export the results in the Tableau project via the Publish as PDF function, via **File → Print to PDF**.

   a. This is a very easy way to transfer Tableau results to people without Tableau.

   b. Unfortunately, unless you have purchased Adobe Acrobat (not just the free Reader version), you will not be able to edit and rearrange the results exported via this method.

4) Individually copy and paste views from Tableau to other applications, such as Microsoft PowerPoint and Word, via **Worksheet → Copy → Image or by right-clicking over the view and selecting Copy → Image.**

   a. This is flexible and works across many Windows applications. The image is of high quality for general-purpose presentations.

   b. If you want to update a slide deck or Word document on a frequent basis, there is no automation method for this task, so you will need to copy it each time from Tableau.

5) Use the "dashboard" functionality in Tableau to combine multiple views created in a Tableau project into one unified "dashboard" view. Access this capability via **Dashboard → New Dashboard**. We teach you how to build a basic dashboard near the end of the book.

Chapter 4

Core view types in Tableau

Chapter Highlights

- Understand the core view categories

    o   Tables—when the details are the point

    o   Bar Charts—the most flexible and easy-to-understand views

    o   Line Charts—display what happened over time

    o   Percent-of-Total—contribution of categories to the overall amount

---

Views are the foundation of Tableau, so mastering them is the key to optimizing your analysis. This chapter is an introduction to the core view types.

Use the Show Me dialog to display the array of twenty-three specific view types. Tableau automatically highlights the view that it "guesses" will be the most useful for the data items that you selected, and lets you know which other views are available. Views that are not appropriate due to the nature of your selected data items are grayed out on the Show Me dialog.

If you accept the Show Me view, you can easily change the view type later via Show Me or by your own manual modifications to the shelves and settings. In fact, when you manually adjust your view, Tableau may surprise you by automatically changing it to the one you wanted.

We have grouped the twenty-three view templates into ten logical categories. This chapter reviews the first four view categories: tables, bar charts, line charts and percent-of-total charts. First, a summary chart displays these four categories, which contain twelve of the templates from Show Me, along with a thumbnail picture and the data items that we suggest to create that view type (these may differ from those suggested in the software). After the summary chart, a description with example is included for each view type.

For more general information on choosing the right view types and best practices for visual analytics, read our book ***The Accidental Analyst: Show Your Data Who's Boss***. Executives at Tableau were so excited about drafts of the book that they purchased a pre-publication copy for every attendee of their Customer Conference in October 2011.

View Category Name	View Example	Suggested Dimension Items	Suggested Measure Items
Table text tables (cross-tabs)		1 or more (may be 0 if have at least 1 measure)	1 or more (may be 0 if have at least 1 dimension)
Table highlight tables		1 or more	1
Table heat maps		1 or more	1 or 2
Bar Chart horizontal bars		0 or more	1 or more
Bar Chart stacked bars		2 or more	1 or more
Bar Chart side-by-side bars		1 or more	2 or more
Bar Chart histogram		0	1
Bar Chart bullet graphs		1 or more	2

View Category Name	View Example	Suggested Dimension Items	Suggested Measure Items
Line Chart continuous lines		1 date or 1 continuous	1 or more
Line Chart discrete lines		1 date and 1 optional dimension	1 or more
Percent-of-Total pie charts		1 or more	1 or 2
Percent-of-Total treemaps		1 or more	1 or 2

Tables—an eye for detail

Tables are great for displaying counts or measures relative to categorical variables. They are useful for looking up individual data point values and for comparing them across one or more levels of dimensional detail. Tables often are called crosstabs or pivot tables.

There are three table views in Tableau: text tables (crosstabs), highlight tables, and heat maps.

Text tables

Text tables are the best choice when you need to reference specific values for data precision and data checking. They are the most familiar view for Excel users. Text tables are very flexible in Tableau and can easily morph into other view types, so if you want to review detailed data values before moving on to other view types, they are a good starting point.

! Performance Tip: There is no need to add every field to the text table. Rather, start with a summary containing just a few crucial dimensions and then drill into the interesting areas by filtering and adding more detail when needed.

A text table excerpt showing *Profit* and *Profit versus Plan* by *Market, Product, Year* and *Quarter*

Market	Product		2012 Q1	2012 Q2	2012 Q3	2012 Q4	2013 Q1	2013 Q2	2013 Q3	2013 Q4
Central	Darjeeling	Profit	$1,050	$1,155	$1,220	$970	$1,583	$1,630	$1,722	$1,439
		Profit vs Pl..	$20	$35	$70	$80	$553	$510	$572	$549
	Earl Grey	Profit	$991	$1,075	$1,073	$1,070	$1,495	$1,520	$1,518	$1,592
		Profit vs Pl..	$81	$55	$63	$180	$585	$500	$508	$702
	Green Tea	Profit	$77	$87	$130	$205	$117	$122	$184	$305
		Profit vs Pl..	($13)	($3)	($10)	($5)	$27	$32	$44	$95
East	Darjeeling	Profit	$645	$676	$710	$618	$973	$957	$1,002	$919
		Profit vs Pl..	($195)	($184)	($210)	($182)	$133	$97	$82	$119
	Earl Grey	Profit	$290	$327	$377	$394	$437	$461	$534	$584
		Profit vs Pl..	($60)	($53)	($43)	($46)	$87	$81	$114	$144
	Green Tea	Profit	$545	$612	$625	$525	$819	$866	$883	$779
		Profit vs Pl..	($155)	($138)	($155)	($145)	$119	$116	$103	$109
West	Darjeeling	Profit	$1,143	$1,167	$1,271	$1,219	$1,725	$1,650	$1,798	$1,811
		Profit vs Pl..	$223	$207	$251	$299	$805	$690	$778	$891
	Earl Grey	Profit	$1,002	$1,120	$1,192	$940	$1,512	$1,580	$1,685	$1,395
		Profit vs Pl..	$192	$230	$192	$260	$702	$690	$685	$715
	Green Tea	Profit	($666)	($702)	($833)	($695)	($1,009)	($993)	($1,184)	($1,030)
		Profit vs Pl..	($356)	($322)	($393)	($295)	($699)	($613)	($744)	($630)

An excerpt of the same text table, filtered by *Market* and color-encoded by *Product*

Product
- Darjeeling
- Earl Grey
- Green Tea

Market	Product		2012 Q1	2012 Q2	2013 Q1	2013 Q2
Central	Darjeeling	Profit	$1,050	$1,155	$1,583	$1,630
		Profit vs Plan	$20	$35	$553	$510
	Earl Grey	Profit	$991	$1,075	$1,495	$1,520
		Profit vs Plan	$81	$55	$585	$500
	Green Tea	Profit	$77	$87	$117	$122
		Profit vs Plan	($13)	($3)	$27	$32

Highlight tables

Highlight tables are useful for emphasizing the range of values in a table by using color, while still allowing easy access to the detailed values.

A highlight table showing
Profit as a % of Plan by Product Type for Year and Quarter

	2012				2013			
	Q1	Q2	Q3	Q4	Q1	Q2	Q3	Q4
Coffee	72%	74%	74%	70%	109%	104%	105%	104%
Espresso	79%	80%	79%	73%	119%	113%	112%	109%
Herbal Tea	85%	88%	87%	91%	128%	125%	122%	136%
Tea	95%	97%	96%	103%	143%	137%	136%	153%

Profit as a % of plan

70%   130%

In the following table, notice how quickly you can see that 2012 was much less profitable relative to plan than 2013. Coffee was the worst relative performer in both years, and Tea was the best relative performer in both years.

Heat maps

Heat maps enable easy comparison of categorical values using color ranges. Use these when the specific values are less important than quickly identifying the trends based on the intensity or "temperature" of a measure, or when you have many members in several dimensions (e.g., all product sales and profits in all zip codes). The layout is similar to a text table with variations in values encoded as colors.

A heat map showing *Profit as a % of Plan* (color-encoded) and *Sales* (size-encoded) by *Product* and *Market* for *Year* and *Quarter*

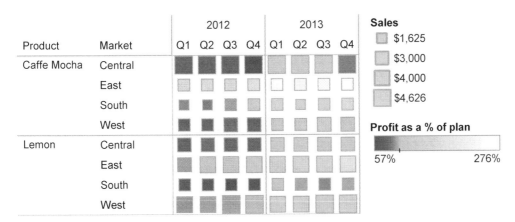

In this heat map, you can quickly see a wide array of information. For instance, Central was the biggest seller of Caffe Mocha (size of square). Caffe Mocha in the East was the only product to hit the profit plan target throughout 2012 (lighter squares in the illustration). Lemon in the East had high sales and was above profit plan target in all quarters except for Q1 of 2012 (size and color of squares, respectively).

Bar Charts—five flavors to meet your needs

Bar Charts are the most flexible of the chart types and useful for almost any visual analysis that involves categories or dimensions but does not require the details of a text table—from dimensional comparisons to data ranking to data distribution to time series. As a bonus, bar charts are also very easy to comprehend since the human visual system is quite effective at understanding and rapidly comparing bar lengths. The five types of bar charts in Tableau are *horizontal bars*, *stacked bars*, *side-by-side bars*, *histograms* and *bullet graphs*.

Since bar charts encode the data values by the length of the bar, bar charts have one key constraint: they must show the zero value on your measure axis or the analysis will be misleading. Tableau automatically displays the zero value for you.

Horizontal bars

Horizontal bars are useful for displaying one or more measures across a dimension. Even if multiple measures are graphed using different scales or units of measure, you still can compare the overall shape and trend of the bars. This illustration is a simple horizontal bar chart, with the length of the bars representing sales and profit for each product.

Horizontal bar chart for *Sales* and *Profit* by *Product*

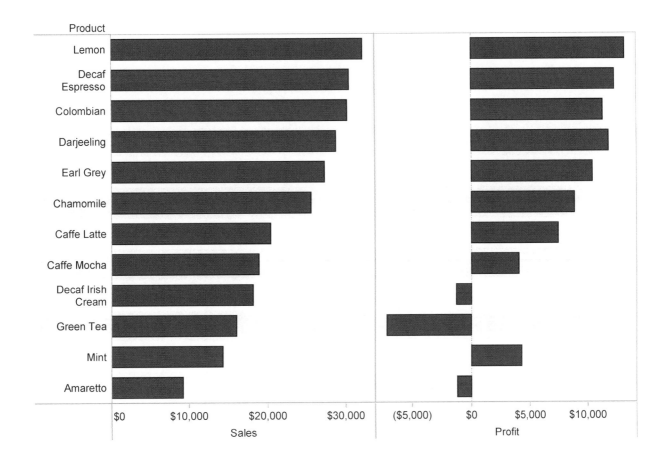

We sorted the bars by descending sales for easy comparison. Note that some of the bottom-selling products have negative profit!

A more complex alternative of the horizontal bar chart is a bar chart with an additional measure on the color button. In addition to the related primary measure (bar length), color encoding can be useful for understanding intensity of a measure. In the following view, we added *Profit Margin* in color to the previous chart.

The same bar chart with *Profit Margin* in color

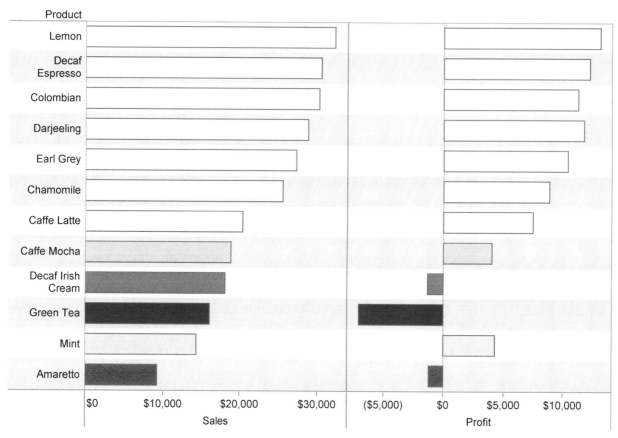

Profit margin as % of sales
-44% ▮▮▮ 44%

As a percent of sales, the low margin products are the darker ones, with the lowest the darkest, and the high margin products are grey to white, with the highest being white. Note that the top seven items in both sales and profit also have the highest profit margin as a percent of sales, which is good. Perhaps the items at the bottom of the graph with low sales, profit and profit margin as a percent of sales, such as Decaf Irish Cream, Green Tea and Amaretto should be removed from the menu. Although Mint is relatively low in sales and profit, the profit margin is high so it may be worth retaining.

Stacked bars

Stacked bars are useful for showing the overall trend across categories or over time while simultaneously comparing the trend within categories for absolute measures. If you have a horizontal bar chart with many categories that requiring extensive scrolling to review, a stacked bar chart can be a good alternative.

A stacked bar chart of *Profit* by *Quarter* and *Market*; filtered by Caffe Mocha and Regular Expresso

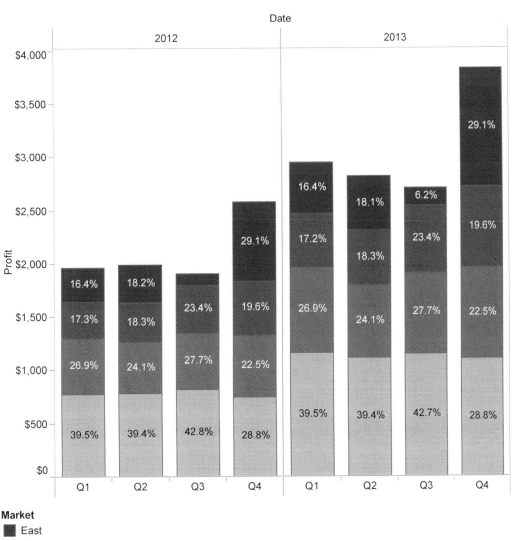

Overall, profit peaked in Q4 for both years, and increased for all four quarters in 2013 relative to 2012. In general, the highest percentage of profit was generated in the Central market, although the East had a slightly higher percentage of profit in Q4 of both years.

Side-by-side bars

While horizontal bars are generally superior, *side-by-side bar charts* can be useful when comparing similar measures within each cell.

**A side-by-side bar chart of *Profit* and *Profit versus Plan*
by *Year* and *Product Type***

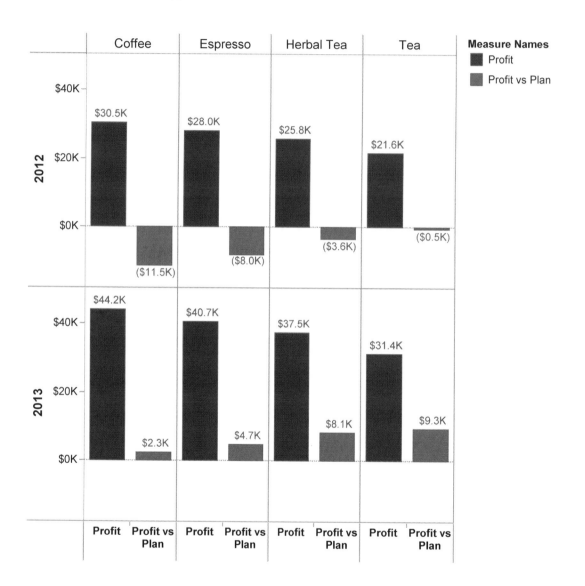

In both 2012 and 2013, Coffee had higher profit than Espresso, which had higher profits than Herbal Tea. Tea had the least. However, profits were up across the board in 2013 compared to 2012. In 2012, profits always fell short of planned profits. In 2013, planned profits were met for all four products.

Histogram

A *histogram* is a specialized bar chart that displays frequencies of a value or range of values. By convention, these are usually vertical (up and down) bars. A histogram is useful for examining the distribution of occurrences.

A histogram of metropolitan umemployment rates for June 2011

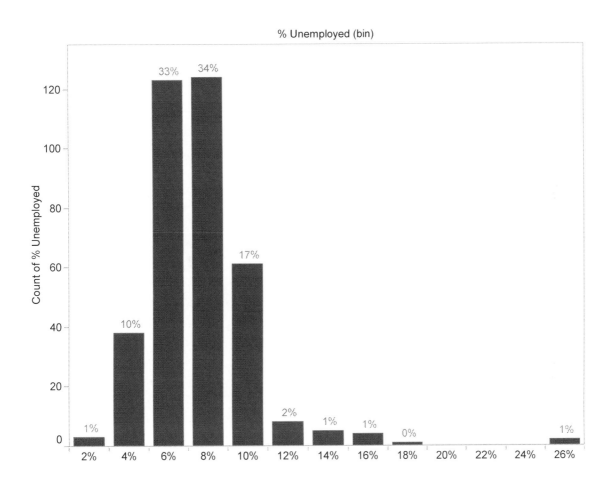

Three-hundred cities are included in these counts. Two-thirds of cities were in the **6-8%** range of unemployment rates.

Bullet graphs

A *bullet graph* is a cool alternative to using dashboard gauges or meters to indicate how close you have come to attaining a goal. This is a cutting-edge graph type developed by data visualization expert Stephen Few. It displays a lot of information in a compact area, yet it is easy to read (once you understand how it works). You can use bullet graphs if you have a dimension and two related measures—an actual measure, such as *Profit*, and a target measure, such as *Budget Profit*.

A bullet graph with *Profit* by *State*—the target is *Budget Profit*

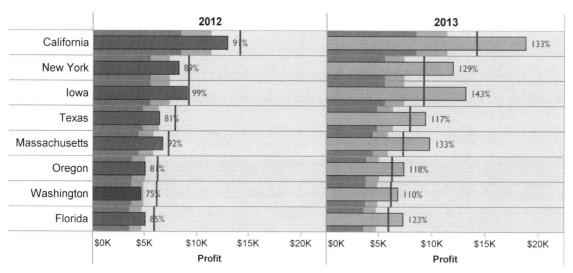

Profit plan achievement
- 100% or more of plan
- 80-99% of plan
- 60-79% of plan

The horizontal bar is the "bullet", *Profit* in this example, shown by *State*. The small, black vertical line is the "target", *Budget Profit*, the planned profit for each state by year. This graph is sorted in descending order by *Budget Profit*, to emphasize the state with the highest targets. The bars are color-encoded, depending upon how close each state's actual profit is to the planned profit. Note that none of the states achieved their target in 2012 but most did in 2013!

One last element of the bullet graph is for quick reference—the area behind the bars shaded in dark gray indicates 0-60% of the target, the range from the dark gray to the mid-gray areas indicates 60-80% of the target and the light gray area is 80% and above the target. These percentages can be changed.

! *Performance Tip:* Since Tableau is unaware of whether a particular measure is a target or an actual value, it may place the items in the wrong position for your bullet graph. The target should appear on the Detail button. If you need to swap the measures, right-click on the horizontal axis and select Swap Reference Line Fields. If you attempt to swap them by manually dragging and dropping the fields, you will lose key elements of the bullet graph, which you will need to add back manually!

Line Charts—display what happened over time

When a dimension field includes a date, Show Me recommends a **line chart** because it is more effective than a bar chart for showing trends across multiple categories. There are two types of line charts: *continuous* and *discrete*. Although discrete is Tableau's default line chart for reasons that we discuss with that view, first we cover continuous lines because more people are familiar with this view type.

Lines (continuous)

Continuous line charts are useful at exploring the relationship of two continuous measures as shown below. While date data items can be used with this chart type, it may be useful to use a discrete line chart (shown next) instead of a continuous line chart for easier comparison of specific time periods.

A continuous line chart showing *Sales* per *Month* categorized by *Ship Mode*

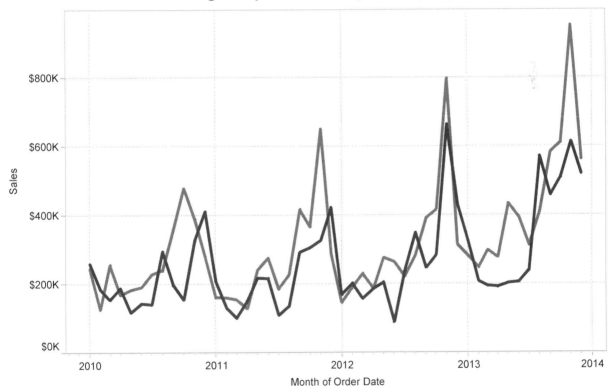

Ship Mode
■ Delivery Truck
▨ Regular Air

Note several interesting points about the peak months of Delivery Truck and Regular Air sales. In 2010, sales peaked for Delivery Truck mode in December and for Regular Air mode in October. In 2012 and 2013, peak sales for Delivery Truck mode moved slightly earlier in the year while those for Regular Air moved later in the year. In 2012 and 2013, Delivery Truck and Regular Air sales peaked in the same month. Also, peak sales for Delivery Truck mode were much lower in 2011 and 2013 relative to the peak of Regular Air in 2010 and 2012.

73

Lines (discrete)

Discrete line charts are useful for showing trends over time across one or more categories. Use them if you need to quickly and easily compare similar time periods such as Q1 of this year versus Q1 of last year. The default is to treat the date dimension as a discrete variable, meaning that the next highest level of date data is used to break the lines into sections in the chart. Note that the default date view is shown at the year level of detail. If you drill down to quarter, the view is broken into sections by year.

A discrete line chart of *Profit* by *Month* for 2012-2013, with *Coffee Type* in color

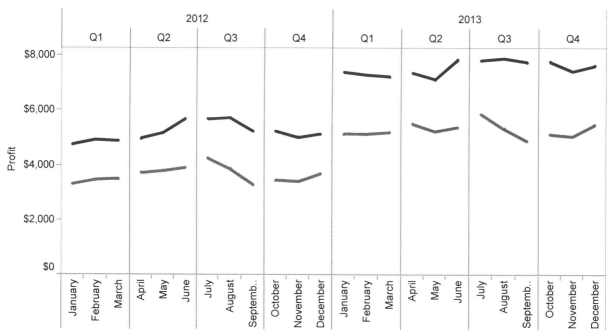

Type
■ Regular
■ Decaf

In the example, overall coffee profits are higher year over year for both Regular and Decaf, which also can be detected in a continuous line chart. However, the discrete line chart clearly shows which quarters in 2013 have different patterns relative to 2012. For example, in Q2 of 2013, the shape of the lines change for both Regular and Decaf when compared to Q2 of 2012.

Percent-of-Total—contribution of categories to the overall amount

Percent-of-total charts display how particular categories comprise the total amount of a measure, and also are referred to as relative contribution or part-to-whole charts. The goal is to quickly compare categories to get a sense of how important they are relative to one another. The two types of percent-of-total graphs in Tableau are *pie charts* and *treemaps*, although some variations of bar and area charts can be used for similar purposes and often are better choices to convey this type of information.

Be careful when using percent-of-total charts, as they have several limitations which can be quite serious. Accurate comparisons can be difficult to make because the measure is represented by area which is two-dimensional, rather than the height of a bar, which is one-dimensional. Averages, minimums, maximums, and other non-additive statistics in pie slices or treemap sections will be very misleading. Measures with negative values are rarely appropriate because it's not useful to have a negative pie slice or section, so avoid them at all costs. Also, too many slices or sections clutter the view and obscure the information.

Pie charts

Tableau having a *pie chart* view is akin to chickens having a pet hawk—much unexpected! Tableau added this view type due to popular customer demand, in spite of the well-known minimal utility of this view type. Both Edward Tufte and Stephen Few (highly respected experts in data visualization) are against the overuse of this chart type and with good cause—they are frequently misleading and inappropriate for effectively conveying information. Unfortunately, they are popular in business applications due to their "appetite" appeal—after all, who doesn't like pie? The easiest fallback from a pie chart habit is a bar chart, which is typically superior at conveying the information in your data.

A good rule to remember with pie charts is to limit the number of slices shown to five or less. If you have more than five slices, you should use the grouping capability of Tableau to reduce the less important slices past the top four into one "Other" slice.

Given the limitations, the example below shows a relatively useful application of pie charts, but one that is rarely used. It shows *Profit* of an office equipment firm across *Region*, *Product Category*, and *Customer Segment*—with the overall size of the pie conveying the overall profit level at the intersection of *Region* and *Product Category*. Additional clarity is added by sorting all three dimension items by descending sum of profit. Also, we've demonstrated the issue with negative values at the pie size level below using profitability.

A grid of pie charts showing *Profit* (overall pie size)

by *Region, Product,* and *Customer Segment*

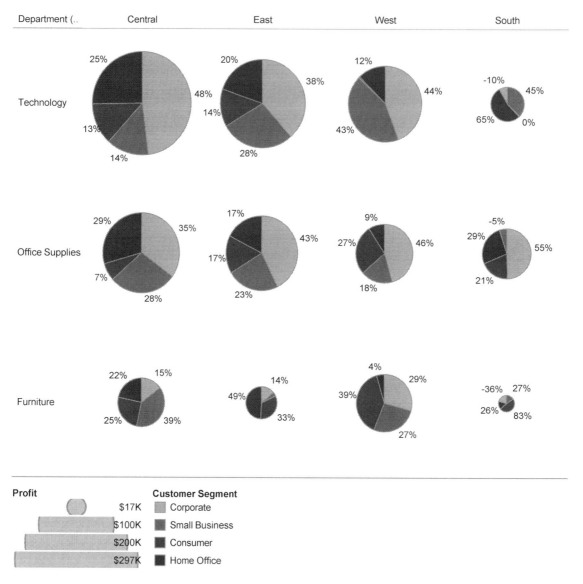

It is easy to see that the Central region has the most profitable product line with technology products, since it is the largest pie, and that corporate customers are the most profitable in more than half of the region/product intersections, as the light corporate "slices" are the largest.

One oddity is the fact that the South/technology intersection has negative profitability! How can a pie be a negative size since the area of the pie conveys the relative contribution of the pie? Tableau attempts to overcome this deficiency of pie charts by making the pie nearly invisible, which is a good compromise if you must use pie charts, but the best solution would be to use a different view type, such as a bar chart.

Treemaps

Treemaps are a compact way to display a large amount of part-to-whole information and look like a collage of variously sized and colored rectangular tiles. In their simplest form, they are composed of sections that display both a primary categorical level of a measure in size and color to provide an overall picture and a secondary categorical level of that measure in size for detail, with both levels independently adding up to 100%. The only aggregates that should be used with treemaps are additive aggregates such as sum, count and count distinct.

They can be extremely complex and there has been a lot written about them in the world of data visualization, complete with specialized terminology. Here we cover only the basics—please consult a reference for details on advanced applications of treemaps.

Here is a treemap depicting *Profit* by *Region* and *Department*. Note that the tiles are labeled with detailed information, which can be adjusted. Color represents the department, the region is simply written in the text, and profit is represented by size in addition to the text and expressed as both percent of total profit and percent of each department's profit.

A treemap displaying *Profit* by *Department* and *Region*

Central Technology $297K (23% of total) 44% of Technology	East Technology $209K (16% of total) 31% of Technology	Central Office Supplies $167K (13% of total) 37% of Office Supplies	West Office Supplies $84K (6% of total) 18% of Office Supplies

East Office Supplies $143K (11% of total) 32% of Office Supplies

South Office Supplies $58K (4% of total) 13% of Office Supplies

West Technology $148K (11% of total) 22% of Technology

South

West Furniture $79K (6% of total) 45% of Furniture

Central Furniture $55K (4% of total) 31% of Furniture

East Furniture $26K (2%

South Furniture

Department
- Furniture
- Office Supplies
- Technology

In this treemap, Technology is the dominant Department, with more than half of total sales. Office Supplies is second with approximately one-third of sales. Furniture comprises the balance. The West region has the widest range of department contributions with 45% of Furniture sales, 22% of Technology sales and only18% of Office Supplies sales.

For detailed information on how to best utilize many of the chart types included in this chapter, complete with expert tips and tricks, read our book, ***The Accidental Analyst: Show Your Data Who's Boss***, available on Amazon. Although the content of the book is not tied to any particular software, many Tableau users consider it a great additional reference when analyzing their business data.

Now it is time to move onto more advanced chart types!

For more possibilities with treemaps, visit www.freakalytics.com/rgts8 and watch our videos on Better Analytics with Tableau 8. This video has an accompanying sample workbook so you can follow along at your own pace, if you like.

Chapter 5

Advanced view types in Tableau

Chapter Highlights

- Understand the six advanced view categories in Tableau

    o   Scatter plots—explore relationships

    o   Circle plots—go beyond bar charts

    o   Maps—great for location data

    o   Area charts—track multiple groups over time

    o   Dual charts—compare two measures on two vertical axes

    o   Gantt Chart—track activity over time

Views are the foundation of Tableau, so mastering them is the key to optimizing your analysis. In the last chapter, you learned about the core view types. This chapter explains the advanced view types.

Use the Show Me dialog to display the array of twenty-three specific view types. Tableau automatically highlights the view that it "guesses" will be most useful for the data items that you selected, and lets you know which other views are available. Views that are not appropriate due to the nature of your selected data items are grayed out on the Show Me dialog. If you accept the Show Me view, you can easily change the view type later via Show Me or by your own manual modifications to the shelves and settings.

We have grouped the twenty-three view templates into ten logical categories for your convenience. This chapter reviews the six advanced view categories: scatter plots, circle plots, maps, area charts, dual charts and Gantt charts. First, a summary chart displays these six categories, which contain eleven of the templates from Show Me, along with a thumbnail picture and the data items required to create that view type. After the summary chart, a description with example is included for each view type.

For more general information on choosing the right view types and best practices for visual analytics, read our book ***The Accidental Analyst: Show Your Data Who's Boss***. Many Tableau users have found the book useful and analytics professionals such as Stephen Few and organizations including TDWI recommend it.

View Category / Name	View Example	Suggested Dimension Items	Suggested Measure Items
Scatter Plot		I or more	2 or 3
Circle Plot circle views		I or more	I or more
Circle Plot side-by-side circles		I or more (at least 3 dimensions /measures in total)	I or more (at least 3 dimensions /measures in total)
Circle Plot packed bubbles		I or more	I or 2
Map symbol maps		I or more geo dimensions;0 or more other dimensions	I or 2
Map filled maps		I or more geo dimensions;0 or more other dimensions	I

View Category / Name	View Example	Suggested Dimension Items	Suggested Measure Items
Area Chart continuous		1 date; 1 other dimension	1 or more
Area Chart discrete		1 date; 1 other dimension	1 or more
Dual Chart dual lines		1 date; 0 or more other dimensions	2
Dual Chart dual combination		1 date; 0 or more other dimensions	2
Gantt Chart		1 date plus 1 other dimension	0 or 1

Scatter Plots—explore relationships

Scatter plots are useful for understanding the relationship or correlation of two or more measures and at least one dimension. Here is a basic example of a scatter plot.

A scatter plot of Average Profit by Average Sales across Department

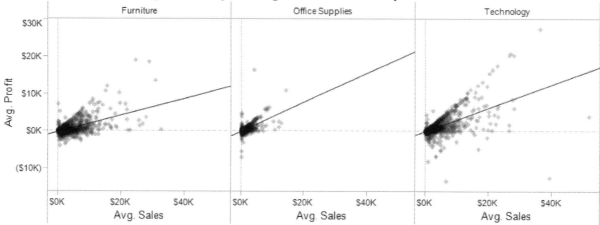

The example contains a lot of valuable information. For instance, the general trend is for average profit to increase with increasing average sales, as indicated by the added trendlines that describe the data. However, in Furniture, average profit is lower for higher avergage sales relative to Office Supplies and Technology. The relationship between average profit and average sales appears to be more tightly grouped for Office Supplies than in Furniture, which is more grouped than in Technology.

Circle Plots—go beyond bar charts

If you would like to examine the variability within or between groups in your data in more detail than is displayed by the averages in a bar chart, **circle plots** are a great option. In a circle plot, the bars are replaced by stacks or groups of circles. The three types of circle plots in Tableau are *circle views, side-by-side circles* and *packed bubbles*.

Circle views

The first type of circle plot is a *circle view*. To demonstrate how it differs from a bar chart, first here is a horizontal bar chart that was swapped to vertical.

To display Average Profit by Department, everyone's familiar with bar graphs, but...

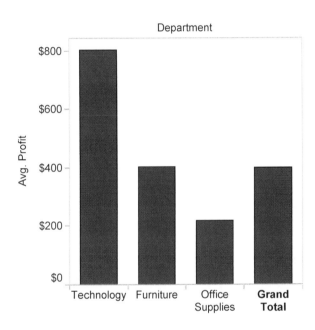

**For more information, use a circle view
of Average Profit by Department with Customer Segment in shape and color**

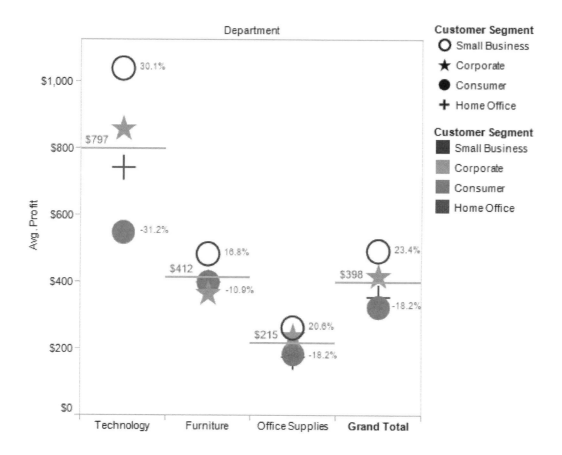

The grey lines represent the average profit for each department, which correspond to the tops of the bars in a bar chart. Beyond that information, the circles display the importance of the four customer segments to each category, and the labels are the percent above or below the average for that particular customer segment (only maximums and minimums are shown). For instance, Technology generates the highest average profit ($797), and small business customers are the greatest contributor to Technology (30% above the average). Consumer customers are the least valuable to Technology (about 31% below average).

Another level of detail added to this circle view to display the variability within each category

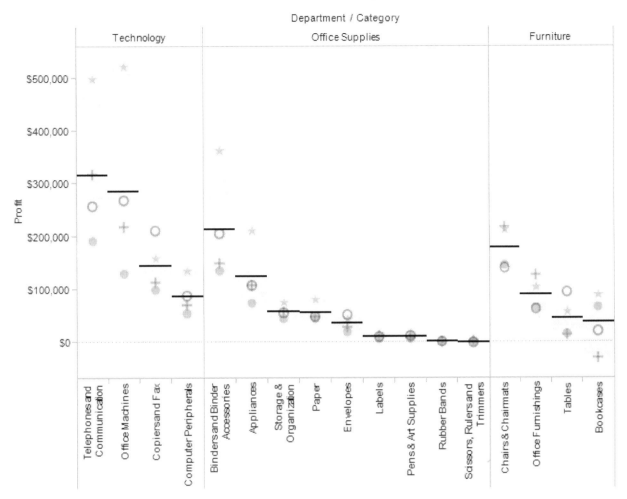

Customer Segment

○ Small Business

● Consumer

★ Corporate

+ Home Office

Now you can really see who is buying what!

Side-by-side circles

The second type of circle plot is a *side-by-side circle*, which are useful to study the difference in two metrics within a category.

A side-by-side circle view comparing Sales and Profit within members of Department

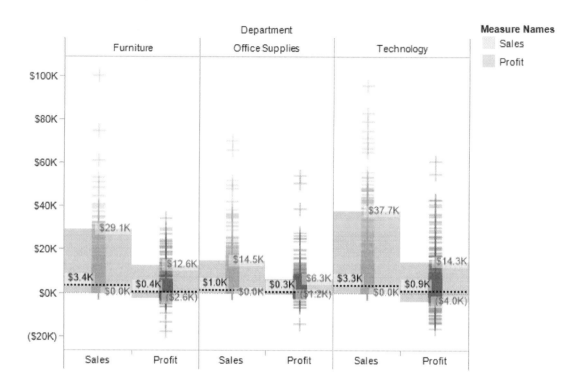

Sales and *Profit* are labeled on the horizontal or x-axis, but they also are color-encoded for emphasis (shown in greyscale here). Averages are the labeled horizontal lines. Note that that you do not have to use circles; you can use other shapes as well (these are plus signs). Each actual sale amount per item ordered is represented by a light plus sign, and the profit is a dark plus sign. This view shows that the highest average sale amount is Furniture, with Technology a very close second. Furniture also has the highest sale ever, more than $100K (it is a faint plus sign!). The highest average profit is in Technology. You wouldn't see this detail in a bar chart!

Packed Bubbles

Packed bubbles charts are appropriate if you have data items that are measured in a non-additive way, such as average, median, maximum and minimum, and you need to quickly find the most important categories. We recommend packed bubbles only for use in compact spaces where a bar chart wouldn't fit, because bar charts and circle views are superior in discerning different sizes of data items. Note that you cannot show negative values, similar to a pie chart.

Here is an example of a packed bubble chart in which *Department* is represented by color, *Category* is on the labels, and *Average Sales* is both on the labels (on the larger bubbles) and encoded in bubble size.

Average Sales *per* Category *with* Department in color

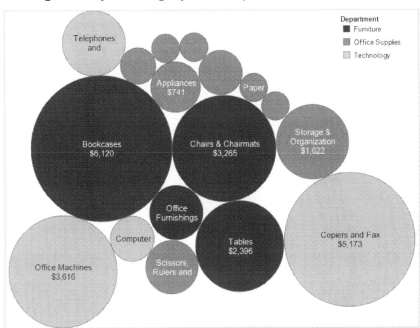

The number of categories are almost evenly split between large, medium and small average sales.

Maps—great for location data

If location is crucial to the problem that you are investigating, display your data on a **map**. Location data include countries, states, counties, cities or postal codes. Maps are interesting and easy to interpret since they are how people naturally think about location data. Tableau has two types of maps: *symbol maps* and *filled maps*.

Symbol maps

Data on *symbol maps* are represented by size- and/or color-encoded shapes.

Symbol map by Country/Region showing
Average Sales size-encoded and Total Profit color-encoded

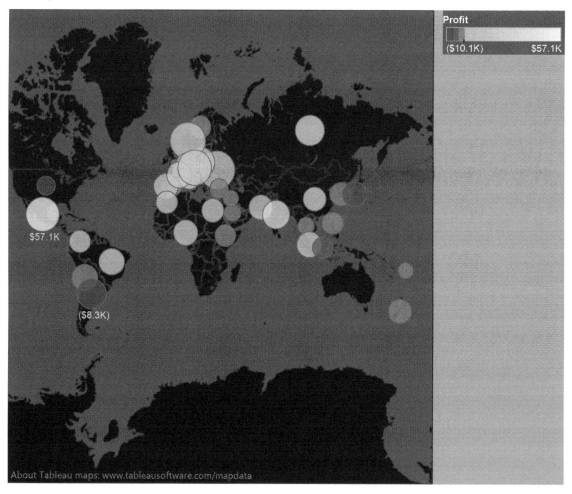

The countries with the highest and lowest profits are labeled. The most profitable country is Mexico, which is white, and also is relatively high in sales, which you can tell from the large bubble size. The least profitable country is Argentina, which is dark in color, and oddly enough is also in the top third in sales, which you can tell from the relatively large bubble size.

Filled maps

Filled maps are useful because people recognize shapes very quickly. If you have one measure, you can fill in regions by shading or color on the map to represent relative intensities of the measure. The upside of the filled map, beyond being easy to understand, is that it is obvious when there are locations with no data. The downside is that smaller locations which may contain important data may go unnoticed and bigger locations that are unimportant may take too much attention. For this reason, filled maps are controversial among data visualization experts.

Filled map with Total Profit color-encoded by Country/Region

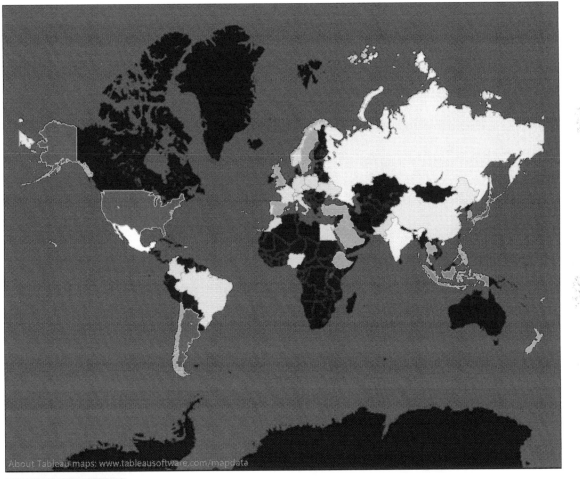

This map uses the same data source as the symbol map, but it can display only one metric. Here *Profit* is shown in color, which appears in greyscale in this illustration. The countries with highest profits are white and the lowest profits are dark.

Area Charts—track multiple groups over time

If you would like to compare how measures within a category change over time relative to one another, an **area chart** may be a good option. Tableau has two types of area charts: *area charts (continuous)* and *area charts (discrete)*.

Area charts (continuous)

Continuous area charts have recently become quite common in the popular media. Here is an example of the simplest type of area chart.

Area chart (continuous) with Sales by Week
Customer Segment color-encoded

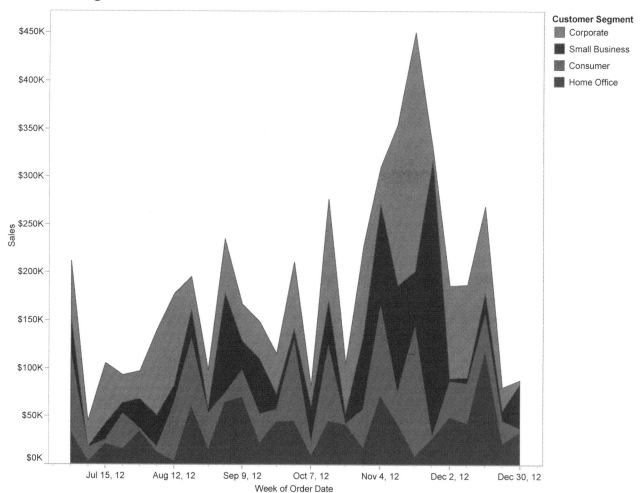

There are several interesting things in this view. Area charts are intended to show a cumulative outcome across categories over time. In Tableau, the colored areas are not in front of each other, they are built upon each other (like the stacked bar chart). Therefore, the value of the lightest area on top equals all four of the differently shaded stacked areas summed together. Note that there are no 3-d effects! Sales are highly volatile (they go up and down a lot).

90

To demonstrate how an area chart displays the data differently from a bar chart, here are the same data in a stacked bar chart.

Bar chart with same data—difficult to track Sales over time for each Customer Segment

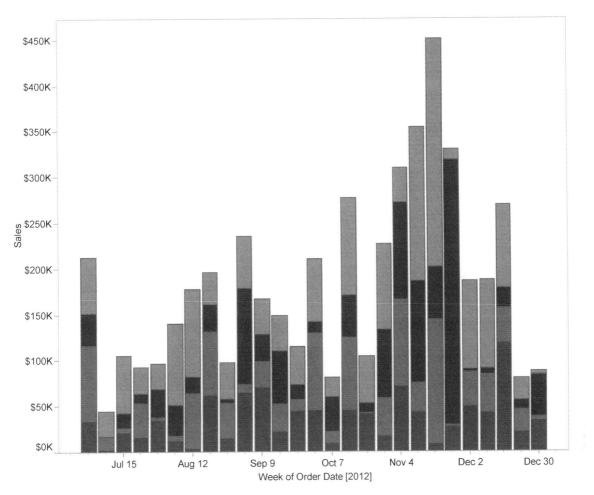

Customer Segment
- Corporate
- Small Business
- Consumer
- Home Office

In the stacked bar chart, you can easily compare the heights of the whole bars to see the overall changes in sales over the 6-month period, but it is difficult to compare the individual stacks between bars to follow the changes in the customer segments. Instead, you tend to look at the stacks in each bar individually. In the area chart, it is much easier to study what happened in the customer segments over time.

Area charts (discrete)

A *discrete area chart* is similar to a discrete line chart. In both view types, time periods are divided into sections for easy comparison of the time periods.

Area chart (discrete) with Percent of Total Sales by Week for 2012 and 2013, color-encoded by Customer Segment

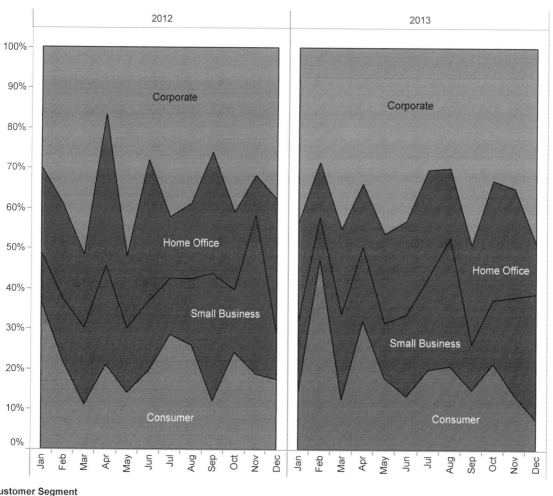

Instead of total sales, sales as a percentage of the whole are plotted on the vertical axis, and 2012 and 2013 are divided into two separate panes in order to compare them. Note that the customer segments are stacked in a different order than in the continuous area chart. In February 2013, there is a peak in the consumer segment. Small business has different peaks in the second half of 2012 versus 2013.

Dual Charts—compare two measures on two vertical axes

Dual charts have two vertical or y-axes and are useful if you have two related measures in the same view space or two or more relevant measures that have different units of measurement (e.g., dollars sold and units sold). Tableau has two types of dual charts available on Show Me: *dual lines* and *dual combination*.

Dual lines

Dual lines charts use color encoding to display the different measurements in the same view area, enabling easy comparison of multiple measures.

The example below contrasts e-mail and printed newsletter sales for a winery over 24 months. For each month, *E-mail Sales* is color-encoded as the dark line and scaled to the left axis, while *Newsletter Sales* is the light line and scaled to the right axis.

Dual lines chart of E-mail versus Newsletter sales

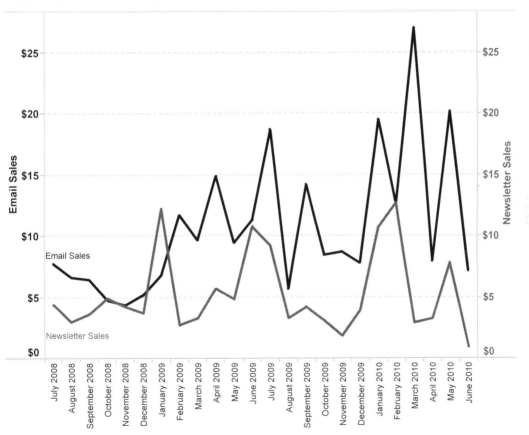

With some modest modifications, even more information can be obtained from this chart. By adding a pane subdivision of the two years by Fiscal Year and adding average reference lines for e-mail and newsletter sales in each year, you can see that e-mail sales are growing aggressively over the two years while overall newsletter sales are flat. Additionally, the monthly variability of both e-mail and newsletter sales appears to be increasing over the two-year period.

By adding panes for each fiscal year and average reference lines, you can quickly obtain more information

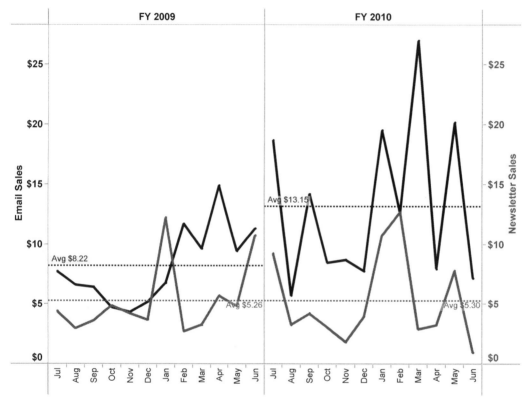

Dual combination

Combination charts allow you to overlay multiple views by combining multiple mark types. The default of this view type is a bar and line chart combination, but you can change this by customizing the marks differently for different measures by right-clicking on the axis for the measure.

This example is the typical usage of the bar-line chart, displaying the relationship between sales and profit.

Bar-line chart with *Sales* on the left axis, shown as bars, and
***Profit* on the right axis, shown as lines**

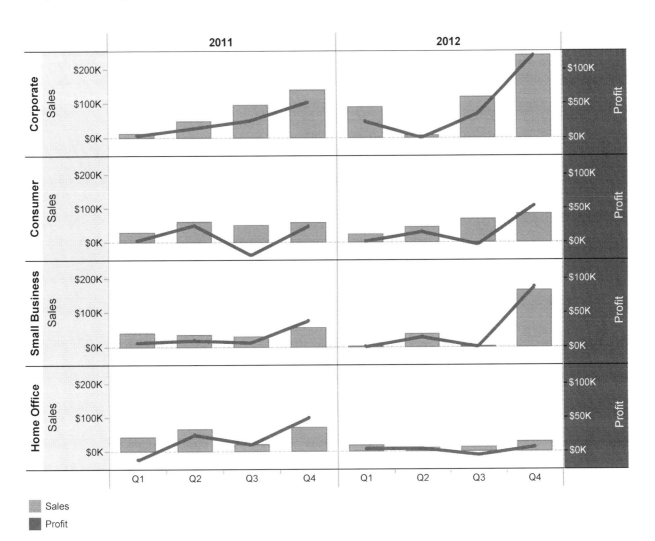

Sales
Profit

Gantt Chart—track activity over time

Gantt charts are a specialized type of chart that can be very useful to track start and end points for an activity over time. Typically, you have to customize these extensively to fit your needs.

This example is a modified Gantt chart. The shipping manager is looking for suspect orders.

**Gantt chart with *Order ID* by *Order Date*,
with *Time to Ship* double-encoded by color and bar length**

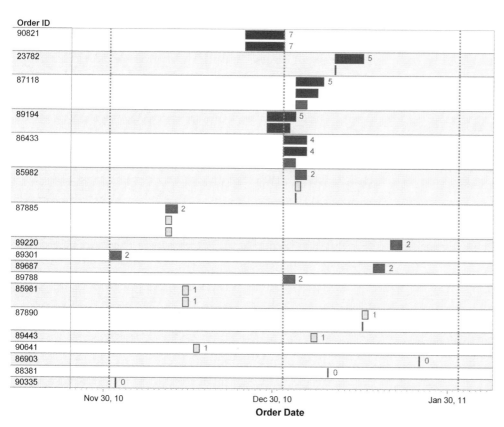

Time to Ship
0.000   8.000

The chart shows the date an order was placed (start of bar) and the dates the individual items within each order were shipped (end of bar). Dark bars are failing expectations of the manager.

Examining this chart yields great insight into quick and slow shipments.

For detailed information on how to best utilize many of the chart types included in this chapter, complete with expert tips and tricks, read our book, *The Accidental Analyst: Show Your Data Who's Boss*, available on Amazon. Although the content of the book is not tied to any particular software, many Tableau users consider it a great additional reference when analyzing their business data.

Chapter 6

Take over with Tableau—View structure, Marks Card, Summaries, Formatting and Titles

---

Chapter Highlights

- Customize views using the Columns, Rows, Pages and Filters shelves

- Enhance your visual appeal with the Marks Card

- The Summary Card—handy description of your data

- Headers and axes

- Titles, captions, field labels, legends

- Format values in your views

This chapter reviews many of the capabilities of Tableau that take you beyond the powerful Show Me defaults and empower you to customize and even build your own views from scratch.

This chapter uses the **Sample—Coffee Chain (Access) dataset**. Throughout the chapter, you will be prompted to return to the original view. To do this, **select the following three data items by keeping the <Ctrl> key depressed:** *Market*, *Product Type* and *Profit*. **Open Show Me and keep the default selection,** *horizontal bars*, **by clicking on it. Hide Show Me. Click the Swap button on the toolbar to flip the bars to vertical.**
Original view: vertical bars displaying *Market*, *Product Type* and *Profit*

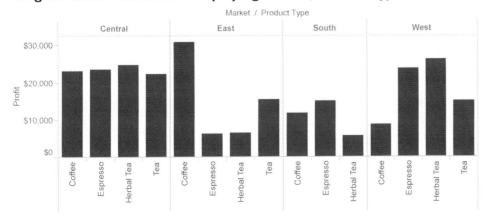

Customize views using the Columns, Rows, Pages and Filters Shelves

In this section, you will learn to manually create or modify views via the Columns, Rows, Pages, and Filters shelves, which are located underneath the toolbar to the right of the Data Items pane.

1. **Columns**: when you place data items on the Columns shelf, such as *Market* and *Product Type* in the default view, you create the vertical column aspect of the view. These data items subdivide the view into vertical columns by determining which values are included on the X-axis (horizontal axis). Starting with the default view, **drag and drop** *Date* **from the Data pane to the right of** *Product Type* **on the Columns shelf.** The chart type automatically changes from *horizontal bars* (remember that you swapped the bars to vertical) to *lines (discrete)*.

! Alternate Route: Move the *Date* field to the first position on the Columns shelf to see a different view of the data. Tableau is all about discovery, so feel free to experiment and move data items around in the examples to see how your insights change!

Date on the Columns shelf

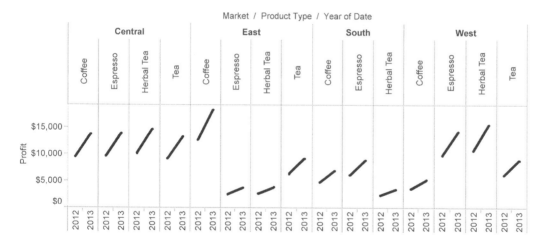

2. **Rows**: determines the values shown horizontally across the rows of the view. Using the Rows shelf, you can partition your chart into horizontal groups by choosing what is included on the Y-axis (vertical axis). **From the Data pane, add** *Market Size* **to the left of** *SUM(Profit)* **on the Rows shelf.**

Market Size on the Rows shelf

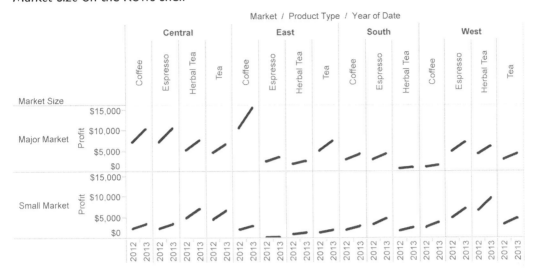

3. **Pages**: if you add a data item to the Pages shelf, you subset the complete view that displays all of the values of that data item into multiple views available on different "pages". The Pages feature allows you to scroll through the various page item values or across time. When you export or print the view, it will only display the currently selected page (similar to a filter, except that the number of rows and columns does not change across pages).

From the Data pane, add *Type* **to the Pages shelf.** Underneath the Pages shelf, the Current Page Card appears, with Decaf displayed in both the drop-down menu and the view. If you click the down caret next to Decaf, you can see that the other available *Type* is Regular. You can change to the Regular view in four ways: **by choosing Regular from the drop-down menu, clicking on the arrow directly to the right, moving the arrow on the progress bar in the middle of the card to the right, or using the scroll bar found on the bottom left of the card.** The three buttons on the bottom right of the card adjust the speed at which the view changes between Decaf and Regular, in case you would like to make visual comparisons between the two.

Data item *Type* on the Pages shelf, page controls below data item
Type on the Pages shelf—Decaf page shown

In contrast with the Filters shelf, placing items on the Pages shelf forces Tableau to examine the data for all available headers across all pages as well as the full range of axis values for every item in the page selection list. Tableau then forces all views to display every header and the full axis range on each page without regard for the currently selected items header and axis range values. Then, using the Pages shelf, you visually can look for gaps and variability among the various items.

4. **Filters:** using the Filters shelf can help you focus on the data that you need and potentially decrease query times by reducing both the data aggregated and retrieved from the data source and the data displayed in the view. For instance, you may only want to look at particular dates, products, or locations and exclude others from the current view. **From the Data pane, add** *Product* **to the Filters shelf.**

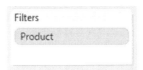

A dialog box will pop up. From the General tab, change the setting from "Select from List" to "Use All" (you could manually specify which products to further filter here, but we want the top 3 overall), then click on the tab labeled Top, select By Field → Top → 3 → Profit → Sum → OK.

Advanced features of the Filter dialog

Product on the Filters shelf

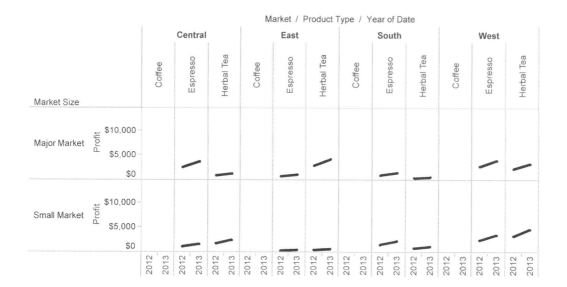

It is important to note that the Filter dialog has a General tab and three additional tabs that interact with the General tab in a specific manner. Item selection on the General tab affects the other tabs. For example, if you select *Lemon* and *Regular Espresso* from the General tab and then request the Top 3 items by Sum of Profit, you will see only two products returned since you selected two items on the General tab.

Additionally, most of the time you will probably select Use All on the General tab and then choose the Top tab for ranking. This is to ensure that all products are automatically included in your Top/Bottom rankings. If you prefer to first select a subset of products and then select a subset of them based on rank, you can return to the first tab and select individual items once you have turned on the Top tab functionality.

Enhance your visual appeal with the Marks card

As shown in previous chapters, the Marks card has a variety of functions that help you build exactly the right view. A mark represents a row (or aggregated group of rows) from your original data source. With the Marks card, you can design the appearance of these marks by placing data items on the Color, Size, Label or Text, Detail, Tooltip, and Path buttons. Additionally, you can place multiple items on the Color, Label or Text, Detail, and Tooltip buttons and the resulting marks incorporate those multiple data items. Note that the Label, Text and Path buttons are specific to certain view types, so they won't always be displayed on the Marks card.

Please reset your view to the original view shown at the beginning of this chapter by opening a new worksheet, selecting *Market*, *Product Type* **and** *Profit*, **opening Show Me, accepting the highlighted view of** *horizontal bars*, **and then hiding Show Me. Swap the bars from horizontal to vertical.**

From the Data pane, place *Market* **on the Filters shelf. When the dialog box pops up, uncheck South and click OK.** This removes South from the view and retains Central, East and West.

! *Alternate Route*: Directly in the view, right-click on South and select Exclude. Alternatively, click on *Market* **on the Columns shelf, select Show Quick Filter and uncheck South on the** *Market* **filter card that appears on the right side of the view.**

1. **Label:** The basic use of the label button is to highlight the same variable or metric with different aggregate values on graphs such as bar charts and maps. You also can change mark label settings including name and font. If you place a data item on the Label button, the item appears on an oval at the bottom of the Marks card. By using the dropdown on the oval, select which type of aggregate value, such as sum, average, count, etc., that you would like to represent a specific variable or metric to summarize data items in charts. Press the Label button to change the mark label settings by interacting with the dialog.

   Drag *Profit* **from the Data Items pane to the Label button.** *SUM(Profit)* **will appear on an oval at the bottom of the Marks card. Click on the down caret that appears when you hover over the oval, scroll down to Measure (Sum) and change the aggregate function from Sum to Average.**

   For more possibilities with the label button, visit www.Freakalytics.com/rgts8 and watch our videos on Better Analytics with Tableau 8. This video has an accompanying sample workbook so you can follow along at your own pace, if you like.

Profit on the Label button; aggregate is Average

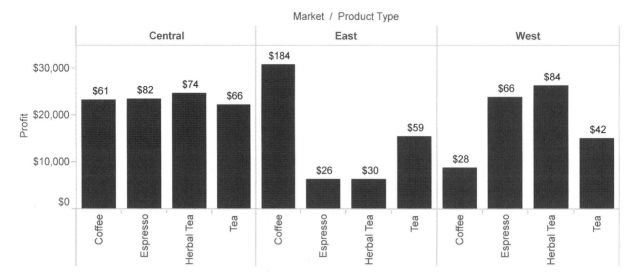

2. **_Text:_** this is very similar to Label, except that it is displayed in place of Label on the Marks Card when your view is a table or cross tab instead of a graph. The dropdown to the right of the data item allows you to select which type of aggregate value that you would like to represent a specific variable or metric to display in tables. The basic use of the text feature is to highlight the same variable or metric with different aggregate values. Pressing the Text button allows you to alter the alignment of the text.

Continuing from the last example, **open Show Me, choose _text tables_ and hide Show Me.** Note that the Label button has turned into the Text button.

The Label button changes to Text for text table views

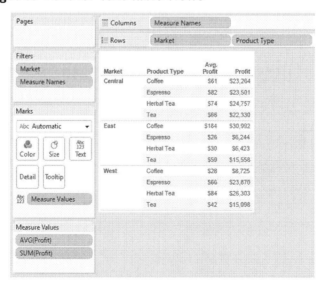

3. Color: this gives you the ability to highlight the view with a range or spectrum of colors for measure items or discrete colors for categorical dimension items. **Type <Ctrl> + Z to undo the last step, returning to the bar chart. Drag** *Market Size* **from the Data items pane to the Color button.** The default colors are assigned from the "Tableau 10" color palette (after adding *Market Size*, the labels moved from the top of the bars to the middle of the bars). To make the colors less dominant in the view, **double-click on one of the colored squares in the color legend.** The Edit Colors dialog appears. **Click on the "Select Color Palette" dropdown in the upper right of the dialog to change the palette to "Tableau 10 Light", then click the Assign Palette button and OK.** The view shows *Profit* for each *Market* and *Product Type* with *Market Size* color-encoded.

Market Size on the Color button

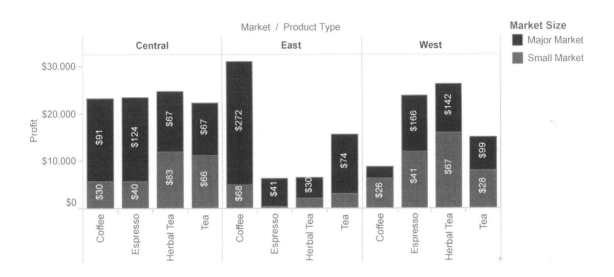

Next, click on the down caret next to Dimensions in the Data Items area and select **Create Calculated Field** from the menu. Name the field "**Profit vs. Budget Profit**". Enter the formula *Profit - Budget Profit* by selecting the two separate measures from the Fields box and adding a minus sign between them. **Drag this new calculated item from the Data Items pane to the color button.** This will replace *Market Size*.

Create and color encode a new calculated field, *Profit vs. Budget Profit*

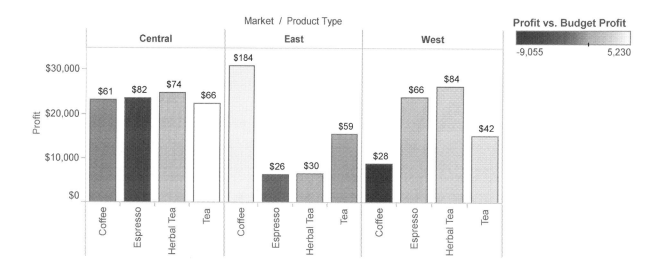

For more possibilities with the color button, visit **www.Freakalytics.com/rgts8** and watch our videos on **Better Analytics with Tableau 8.**

4. **Size:** allows you to alter the size of objects based on the range of values for the selected item. **From the Data items pane, drag** *Sales* **on the Size button.** Note that the widths of the bars change, notably for Espresso, Herbal Tea and Tea in the East market. Size can be a useful means of conveying the relative impact of a related measure on the primary measure. However, note that when comparing the bars visually, bar height is much easier to interpret than bar width.

Sales **on the Size button**

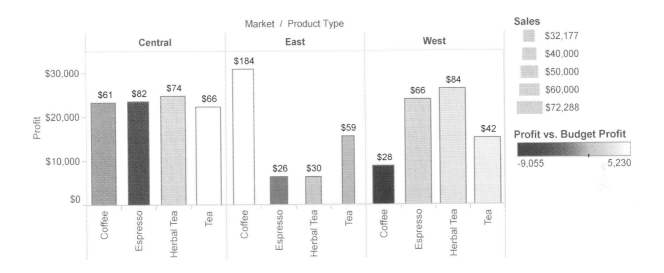

5. **Shape:** you can use this button to control the shapes that display the data from a categorical dimension item. Note that at this point, the Shape button is not displayed on the Marks Card. **Open Show Me, select** *scatter plots* **and then hide Show Me. Move** *Sales* **from the Color button by dragging the** *SUM(Sales)* **oval on the Marks card to the Rows shelf, replacing the item on the Rows shelf. Also, move** *Profit* **from the Size button by dragging the** *SUM(Profit)* **oval to the Columns shelf, replacing that item. Move your mouse to the blank space to the left of the** *Product Type* **oval and a dropdown will appear. Choose Color. Then, swap the rows and columns using the Swap icon on the toolbar.** *Market* **is now shape-encoded and** *Product Type* **is color-encoded. Click on the Shape button to bring up the Edit Shape dialog. Customize the shapes as shown in the illustration.**

Market on the Shape shelf

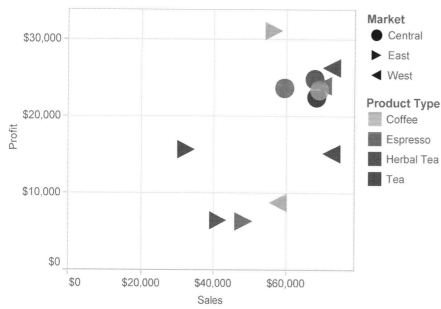

6. ***Detail:*** this button controls the level at which data are summarized in your view. Using dimensional data items, the Detail button allows you to show more levels of information of the data in the view without additional color or shape encoding. This is different from filtering, as it does not exclude data from the view, it simply divides and expands the data marks displayed in your view.

Remove the *Market* **oval from the bottom of the Marks card and the view.** Now *Market* is no longer on the Shape button and the graph has four data points. **Drag** *Product* **from the Data pane to the Detail button.** The data points show each product type (color-encoded) at the product level of detail, so there are now thirteen marks.

Place *Product* **on the Detail button to display an additional level of detail**
Notice the ranges of units change

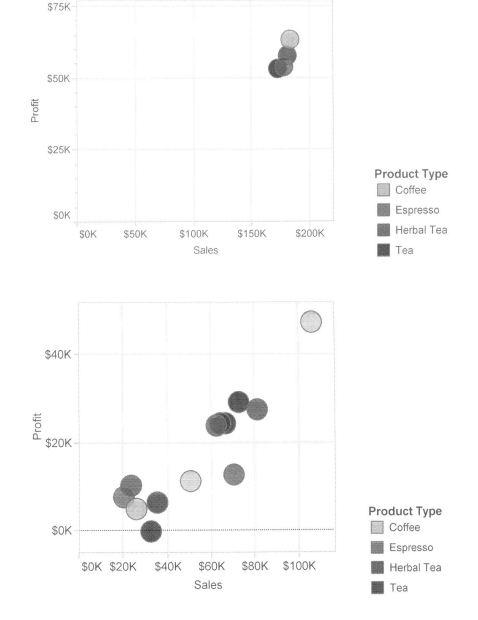

At this point, a product manager may want to emphasize all coffee products to explore how coffee is performing relative to tea for these metrics. **In the Color legend, hold down the <Ctrl> key and click on Coffee and then Espresso.** The selected items are now highlighted both in the legend and in the graph, while all other items are grayed out, enabling easy comparison of coffee and espresso products against tea and herbal tea.

Highlight Coffee and Espresso products only

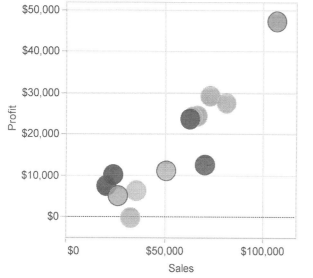

Click on a gray space to release the highlighted items.
Drag *Area Code* **from the Data pane to the Detail button.**

Area Code **on the Detail button**
See more information (more rows and marks displayed)

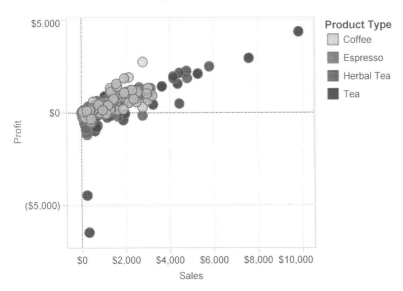

Finally, to show the greatest amount of detail, **use the main menu to turn off all aggregation via Analysis → Aggregate Measures**. Note that once you turn off this option, the Columns and Rows items no longer have aggregate functions in their names, since no aggregation is occurring! **All available data rows will be retrieved from your data source without aggregation, potentially returning an overwhelming amount of data.** Shrink the data points by pressing the Size button and moving the slider that appears all the way to the left. Click in a gray space to hide the slider. Add trend lines by right-clicking on the view and selecting Trend Lines → Show Trend Lines.**

Turn off aggregation, resize the points and add trend lines

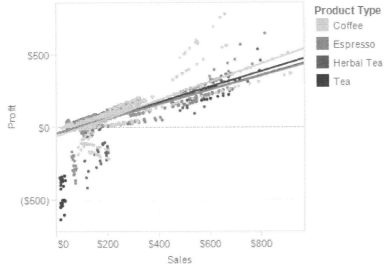

The Summary Card—handy description of your data

The Summary Card describes the measures currently shown in the view. Five summary statistics are listed—Count, Sum, Average, Minimum, and Maximum. If you have data items on the Pages and/or Filters shelves, the Summary Card will show only the data included in the current view. **Turn this on from the main menu by Worksheet → Show Summary.** To copy the summary card values to the clipboard, **click on the dropdown arrow from the card and select Copy.**

Summary Card of all measures in a view

Summary	
Count:	3576
SUM(Profit)	
Sum:	$227,065
Average:	$63
Minimum:	($638)
Maximum:	$778
Median:	$42
SUM(Sales)	
Sum:	$715,885
Average:	$200
Minimum:	$17
Maximum:	$912
Median:	$141

If you would like to summarize certain data points in the view, such as the data in the upper right part of the graph, you can update the Summary Card by selecting the data within the view itself. **Hold the left mouse button down and drag your mouse pointer across the data point region that you want to highlight.** The Summary Card automatically updates the statistics based on the current selection.

Summary Card of measures for upper right part of graph
Note that only the bolded points in the graph are used in the summary

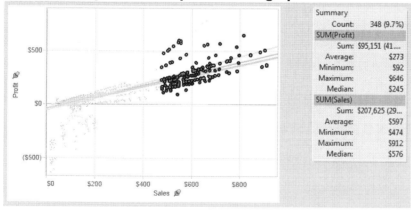

Headers and Axes

Headers and axes are automatically created by Tableau whenever items are placed on the Columns or Rows shelves. By default, a measure is represented by an axis with continuous values and a dimension is represented by a discrete or categorical header. **Please open a new worksheet and reset your view to the original view found at the beginning of this chapter by selecting** *Market*, *Product Type* **and** *Profit*, **opening Show Me, selecting the default view,** *horizontal bars*, **hiding Show Me, and then swapping the horizontal bars for vertical ones.** The figure shows *Profit* (a measure) as a continuous axis and *Market* and *Product Type* (dimensions) as headers.

Profit (measure) as a continuous axis, *Market* and *Product Types* (dimensions) as headers

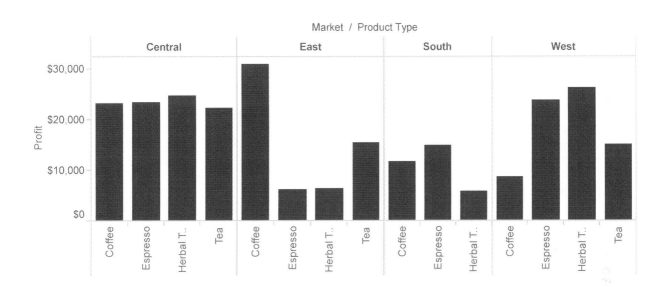

Tableau offers significant control over the layout of axis scales (formatting and appearance of the header and number fonts, orientation, etc. will be covered later in this chapter). **Right-click on the vertical or y-axis labeled** *Profit* **and select Edit Axis.** The Edit Axis dialog appears. Here you can change overall axis range, axis ranges across header groups in columns or rows, scale reversal or logarithmic scaling and tick mark formatting. You also can rename the axis by typing the new names in the title and subtitle fields. As shown in the figure below, **change the range by selecting Fixed and keeping 0 in the Start field and adding 40,000 in the End field. Change the title to "2-Year Total Profits", and click OK to apply the changes and close the dialog**. Note that a pushpin appears near the axis title to remind you that you fixed the range of the axis.

Edit Axis dialog box

You can modify the headers in a similar manner. **Right-click on a header value for** *Product Type* **(Espresso for example) and you will see four options related to the layout of the header:** Format…, Rotate Label, Show Header and Edit Alias. Format allows control over the appearance of the header text and is covered later in this chapter. Rotate Label will rotate the header labels 90 degrees counterclockwise, changing the orientation of the text from horizontal to vertical or vice versa. Show Header controls whether or not the header text is displayed in the view. Edit Alias allows you to give particular values within categorical dimensions new labels to use as headers in the view.

Right-click on the "Herbal Tea" header and select Edit Alias. The Edit Alias dialog appears as shown in the figure below. **Change the Name for Herbal Tea to Decaf Tea, then click OK.** The view updates (shown below).

Rename the alias of Herbal Tea in the Edit Alias dialog box

Modified title on the vertical axis and header alias in the horizontal axis

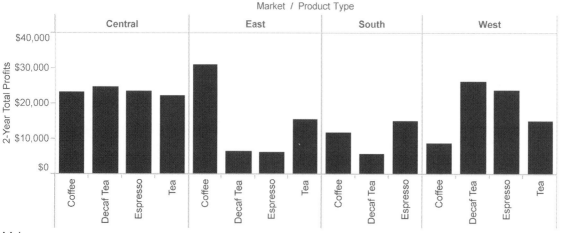

Titles, Captions, Field Labels and Legends

Titles enable quick identification of the content and purpose of your view. By default, the Title is the same as the worksheet name. **Modify the title by selecting Worksheet → Show Title on the main menu to bring up the title shelf, and then double-click on the current title to bring up the Edit Title dialog. Rename the sheet "Stephen".**

Captions typically present more detail about the contents of the view than the Title. Tableau automatically creates a caption based on the view layout, but you can manually modify it. **On the main menu, select Worksheet → Show Caption to place the Caption card in the view. Double-click on the caption or click on the down caret at the right of the Caption card to edit the caption.** In this case, do not change anything so that the default caption will be displayed.

Field labels are the dimension items used to create the headers and automatically are displayed with the headers. For example, in the previous figure in the Header and Axes section, the field label is "*Market / Product Type*". In this case, you can hide the field labels by **right-clicking on** *Market / Product Type* **and selecting Hide Field Label for Columns.**

When data values are encoded by color, shape and/or size, legends are the keys to understanding the encoding. In Tableau, each legend can be customized individually.

To follow the example, code the following data items: **On the Marks card, change the value in the dropdown from Automatic to Shape. Drag** *Market Size* **from the Data pane to the Shape button. Depress <Ctrl>, select the** *Market Size* **oval at the bottom of the Marks card, and drag it to the Color button (a neat little trick to duplicate data items on ovals). Drag** *Marketing* **from the Data pane to the Size button. Simply click on the down caret on any individual Legend shelf and select Edit Colors, Edit Sizes, etc. to customize the legends.**

Change the title, automatic caption as view footnote, hide the field labels, and customize size/shape/color legends

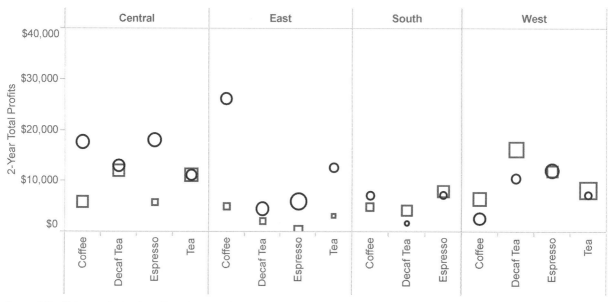

Sum of Profit for each Product Type broken down by Market. Color shows details about Market Size. Size shows sum of Marketing. Shape shows details about Market Size.

Marketing
- $592
- $2,000
- $4,000
- $6,000
- $8,000
- $10,000
- $11,278

Market Size
- ○ Major Market
- □ Small Market

Market Size
- ■ Major Market
- ■ Small Market

Format values in your views

Tableau is extremely flexible and allows you to format all elements in the view. **Right-click on any element in the view and select Format**. The Format dialog appears in place of the Data Items pane on the far left of the screen.

The Format dialog stays visible **until you close it by clicking on the x in the upper right corner of the dialog**. Within the Format dialog, the options vary based on your selected item. For example, in the figure below, the Format dialog on the left side is entitled "Format Product Type". **Click on one of the icons at the top of the format dialog or click on a different item in the view so another element of the view can be edited.** The right side of the figure is the "Format Shading" dialog.

Examples of Format dialog boxes

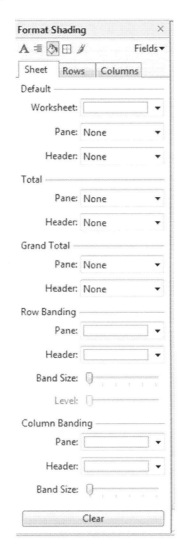

The symbols across the top of the Format dialog represent the various elements that can be formatted. From left to right, the symbols are Font, Alignment, Shading, Borders, and Lines, and on the far right is a dropdown menu for the Fields that you are currently using in your view. Formatting of Font, Alignment, Shading, Borders and Lines can be performed at the overall Sheet, Rows or Columns level. Marks can be formatted only at the overall Sheet level. Formatting can be copied from one sheet to another—even across workbooks. **Right-click on the worksheet tab, select Copy Formatting, right-click on the second worksheet and select Paste Formatting.** Formatting elements can be related to data items, location within the view or the view in general, so be certain to verify the changes you made.

It is easy to format the text of the headers and axes to reproduce the next figure. **Right-click on the vertical axis (2-Year Total Profits) and select Format.** The Format dialog appears. **In the Font field, Worksheet, click on the dropdown to select tan from the color palette.** This changes the font color. **Using the Fields dropdown menu, change the data item to** *Product Type*. **In the Font field, select the italic box to italicize the text.**

Format text of headers and axes

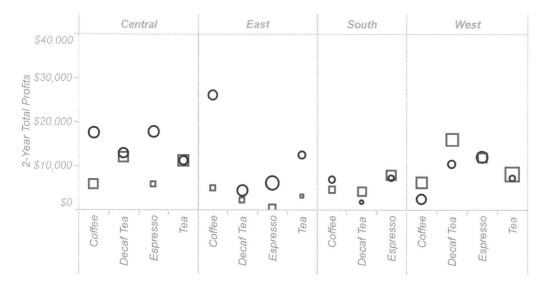

Chapter 7

Organize the data in your Views—Sorting, Filtering, Aggregations, Percentages, Spotlighting, Totals/Subtotals, and Motion Charts

---

Chapter Highlights

- Sort views for quick comparison

- Filter views to find the right information

- Aggregate measures—sums, averages and more

- Use percentages to find the right ratios

- Spotlight your view to emphasize important values

- Add totals and subtotals

- Create a motion chart after connecting to a new data source

---

This chapter covers many of the features in Tableau that control how the data appear in your view once you have added the desired items to the shelves. This includes arranging your view, hiding irrelevant or confusing information, adjusting how measures are calculated, enabling the use of percentages to understand parts of the whole or ratios, spotlighting or calling out certain values, and adding subtotals and totals to your view. At the end of the chapter, you will build a motion chart to track the relationships between your data items over time, using new data. For the first time, you will be connecting to a new dataset that is not included with the software.

This chapter covers a lot of material in-depth, so you might need more time than other chapters to be comfortable with the content.

For most of this chapter, you will use a sample data source provided by Tableau, the **Sample—Coffee Chain (Access)** database. **For the motion chart, you need to download and save a new dataset from the Freakalytics website, the** *Winery customers and sales* **dataset.** It is available at http://www.Freakalytics.com/rgts8

Sort views for quick comparison

Tableau automatically sorts your data along dimensional items used in the view. By default, it sorts the category labels in ascending alphabetical order. For example, Tea, Coffee and Espresso are sorted as Coffee, Espresso and Tea.

It may be useful to sort your view by the measure in use. The quickest way to sort by the measure is **to click on the Sort ascending or Sort descending buttons on the Tableau toolbar**, shown in the figure below.

Sort ascending and Sort descending buttons on the toolbar

For example, you may want to sort your market regions so that they are ordered in the view from highest to lowest profit. **In the Coffee Chain dataset, select** *Market* **and** *Profit*, **unhide Show Me, accept the default** *horizontal bars*, **and hide Show Me.** To see the view on the right, **click on the Sort descending button.** Note that a tiny sort icon appears in the view next to the sorted data item (the icon will not appear when you copy and paste the graph into another document). In this case, if you use the Sort ascending and descending buttons, the sort will update as the data change.

Horizontal bar views with *Profit* by *Market*:
left view—unsorted,
right view—sorted via the Sort descending toolbar button

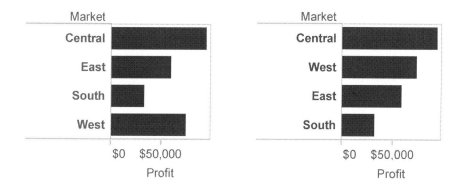

A variety of advanced sorting methods is available beyond the default alphabetic item sorting by dimension and the sort ascending and descending toolbar items by measure. **Right-click on** *Market* **on the Rows shelf and select Sort.** The Sort dialog box appears, which can be used with dimensional items on the Columns or Rows shelf.

From the Sort dialog, you can sort data by the order of the original data source, alphabetically, by any field in your data source, or manually for custom sorting. At the top of the dialog, you can specify either Ascending or Descending order, applicable for alphabetic and field sort options. **In this example, select Sort by Field → *Sales* and click OK** to yield the figure below. This sort results in a different order than descending profit, which is surprising since you would typically expect a strong relationship between sales and profit.

Using the Sort dialog box to Sort by Field

Although you will need to keep *Sales* sorted for the next example, in general all sorting can be cleared by **right-clicking on the dimension item in the Columns or Rows shelf and selecting Clear Sort.**

! *Alternate Route*: You also can directly drag and reorder items in legends or rows and columns to manually sort them. If you manually sort, the data items will remain in that order if the data change. Then, if you pull up the Sort dialog, the Sort order field is grayed out until you select a field.

Filter views to find the right information

Filters reduce the data that are displayed in your view by allowing you to select a subset of the data. Filters can be specified using dimension or measure items, although the two types have different dialogs and options.

The simplest filter uses the labels of dimension items or marks in the view. **To filter by dimension item, right-click on a label or multiple labels in the view and select Keep Only or Exclude. Alternatively, right-click on the data marks themselves or simply hover over them and select Keep Only or Exclude.** Any of these options will create a filter on the dimension item, keeping or excluding the selected items.

To create the next example, **continue from the last example by placing** *State* **on the Color button and** *Profit* **on the Label button**. Filtering of dimension items is also available by dragging the item from the Dimensions pane to the Filters shelf. For example, **drag** *State* **from the Dimensions pane to the Filter shelf**. The Filter dialog appears, as shown in the figure below. There are four tabs available: General, Wildcard, Condition, and Top. The General tab (displayed in the figure) allows selection of the filter criteria by label. **Click None to clear all and select California, Florida and Illinois, and then click OK.**

Filter dialog box with General tab displayed and resulting view

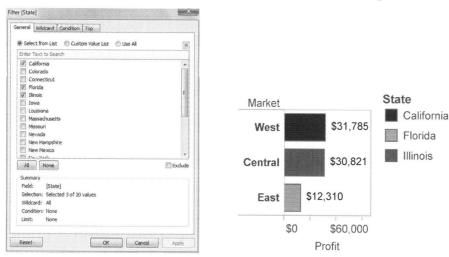

The Condition tab allows filtering the view using any data field with an aggregate function condition such as Sum, Average and Count (aggregations will be discussed in detail later in the chapter). Before switching to the Condition tab, **open the** *State* **filter on the Filters shelf by double-clicking it, and then choose Use All on the General tab. On the Condition tab, choose By Field** → *Sales* → **Sum** → **greater than (>), enter 60,000 and click OK.** This is shown in the next figure.

Filter dialog box with Condition tab displayed and resulting view

To continue with this example, **bring up the** *State* **filter again by clicking on the down caret on** *State* **on the Filters shelf. Click None on the Condition tab, then click on the Top tab.** The Top tab allows you to filter the view using the top or bottom rankings of any data field with an aggregate function condition, such as the ten states with the lowest sales. **Choose By Field → Bottom →10 →** *Sales* **→ Sum and click OK.** This is shown in the next figure with only the Bottom 10 States showing.

Filter dialog box with Top tab displayed and resulting view

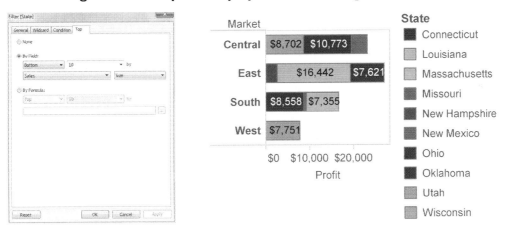

! *Performance Tip*: **A top or bottom filter is applied independent of the other filters in use for a view, so the top/bottom selection will not consider other filters in use unless you add those other filters to the Context (click the other items on the Filter shelf and select Add to Context). A Context Filter is a special type of filter that forces the creation of a temporary database table before proceeding with other filters.**

For more possibilities with data source filters, which will ensure that every view has the same filter, visit <u>www.Freakalytics.com/rgts8</u> **and watch our videos on Better Analytics with Tableau 8.**

Aggregations for measures—sums, averages and more

Tableau automatically assigns an aggregate function to all items that are measures. By default, the aggregate function for non-geographic measures is to *Sum* the data. Each cell or value used to create the view is included when Tableau calculates aggregates. Other common aggregations include *Average* and *Count*. Average is similar to the mean of all the records in a cell and Count is the number of records available in the data source for the cell. Less commonly used aggregations include *Minimum, Maximum, Standard Deviation, Standard Deviation (Population), Variance*, and *Variance (Population)*.

When you use Tableau Data Extracts instead of other local data sources such as Excel or CSV files, two additional aggregates are available: *Median* and *Count Distinct*. The Median is literally the "middle" data value. If you sort all of the values for a data item from lowest to highest, the Median is the value in the middle of this list. The Median is useful if your data item has a few extreme values that may skew the Mean value. For example, you may have sales amounts of $100, $200, $300, $400 and $5,000. The Mean of these numbers is $1,200, but the Median is $300. Notice that the Mean in this case is not close to any actual data value, while the Median is a typical outcome.

Count Distinct is useful for counting the unique names of a data item in your data source. For example, suppose Joe placed 3 orders, Katy placed 8 orders and Patty placed 22 orders. The Count of the data item *First Name* would be 33, but the Count Distinct would be 3, since there are only 3 distinct names in the data item.

In general, you can change the default aggregation from the measures part of the Data shelf **by right-clicking on the item and selecting Default Properties → Aggregation.** Once a measure item is added to the view, you can also customize the aggregation for the current view. **On the shelf where the item is placed, click on the down caret in the oval of the measure item. Select Measure and pick the desired aggregation function.**

Now you will develop an intricate view of three aggregations for the same data item, *Profit*. **Create a new worksheet using the Coffee Chain data source. Duplicate** *Profit* **three times by right-clicking on it directly in the Measures pane and selecting Duplicate. Change the aggregate of the first copy to Average (AVG) by right-clicking on it, selecting Default Properties → Aggregation → Average, and renaming it** *Profit Avg*. **Change the second copy to Maximum (MAX) and name it** *Profit Max*. **Change the third copy to Minimum (MIN) and name it** *Profit Min*.

Place *Market* and *Product Type* on the Columns shelf. On the Marks card, change the dropdown from **Automatic** to **Shape**. Drag *Measure Names* (found in the Dimensions pane) to the Filters shelf. On the dialog, click the **None** button, and then check *Profit Avg*, *Profit Max* and *Profit Min* and then click **OK**. Drag *Measure Names* from the Data pane to the Color button and then a second time to the Shape button. **Add** *Measure Values* (found in the **Measures** pane) to the **Rows** shelf.

Change the colors for *Profit Max* to green, *Profit Min* to red and *Profit Avg* to blue. Change the shapes for *Profit Max* to a down triangle, *Profit Min* to an up triangle, and *Profit Avg* to a filled-in circle. **Format** the *Measure Values* axis to be currency with no decimal places.

Three aggregations of the same measure item, Profit

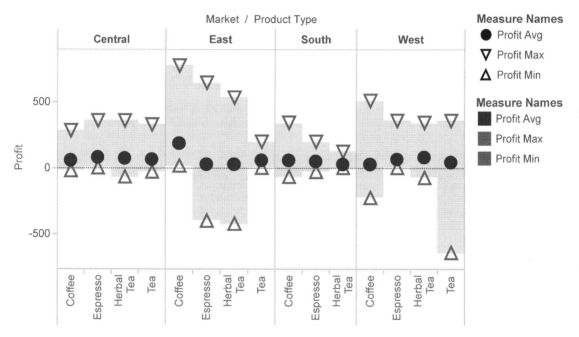

By applying multiple aggregations to the same measure, you can gain additional insights compared to having only a single aggregation view.

Use percentages to find the right ratios

Using percentages in Tableau is easy and informative. Percentages allow the rapid comparison of cells across columns and/or rows when the total amounts vary widely across cells. Percentages can be calculated as a percentage of all values, a percentage of values in a row or column, and a percentage of values in a cell. Other less common percentage calculations are also available.

For the next example, in the Coffee Chain dataset, select *Market, Product Type* **and** *Profit,* **unhide Show Me, accept the default** *horizontal bars,* **and hide Show Me. From the Dimensions pane, drag** *Market* **to the Color button and** *Market Size* **to the beginning of the Columns shelf before** *SUM (Profit).* The profit for each product type in each region and market size is shown in the first view.

Perhaps you are more interested in understanding the relative contribution of each product type to a region/market size. Since various panes where *Region* and *Market Size* intersect have different total profit amounts, it is hard to gauge the relative contribution of each product type to a pane. To simplify this comparison, **from the main menu select Analysis → Percentage of → Pane.** This will change the metric calculation from *Profit* to *Percentage of Total Profit* for a pane, as shown below.

**Profit (left) and Percentage of Total Profit (right)
for each Product Type, by Region and Market Size**

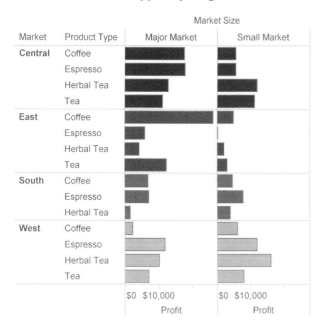 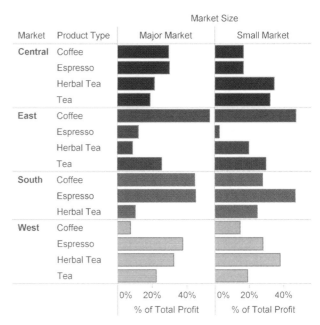

In the original view, overall profits in the South (green in your view) were much lower than the other regions. Once the view was adjusted to show the percentage of profit within each pane, the bars changed based on the total profit in each pane, with each pane totaling 100%. This is very useful if you want to highlight the relative contribution to profit of each product in a particular market.

Spotlight your view to emphasize important values

Spotlighting is a powerful technique in Tableau used to highlight measure values in a table or chart that meet criteria defined by you, typically by color encoding. For example, you may want to highlight products that have profits above $10,000 or below $3,000 to emphasize that they require additional discussion and research. With spotlighting, you can make these products "jump" off the page.

To follow this example, **open a new worksheet, and in Coffee Chain, select** *Market*, *Product Type* **and** *Profit*, **unhide Show Me, accept the default** *horizontal bars* **and then hide Show Me. Move** *Market* **from the Rows shelf to the Columns shelf and from the Data pane, add** *Product* **to the end of the Rows shelf. In the Data Items / Measures pane, right-click on** *Profit* **and select Create Calculated Field.** The Calculated Field dialog appears. **Change the name of the Calculated Field to "Profit Spotlight" and enter the Formula as:**

IF SUM([Profit]) >= 10000 THEN "Best"
ELSEIF SUM([Profit]) <= 3000 THEN "Worst" (Note that the "ELSEIF" function is one word.)
ELSE "Middle of the Pack" END

The dialog should confirm it is a valid calculation, but if an error message pops up, check your formula for typos. **Click OK.** *Profit Spotlight*, the calculated item, will appear in the Data Items / Measures pane. **Double-click on the item and it automatically is added to the Color button on the Marks card.**

Under the Marks card, a color legend card appears. **Double-click on the Best color.** The Edit Colors dialog appears. **Change Best to green, Middle of the Pack to gray, Worst to red, and then click OK. Right-click on South and West in the view and select Exclude.** Only Central and East will be displayed in the view.

Spotlight *Products* with the Best and Worst *Profits*
by color encoding (only Central and East markets shown)

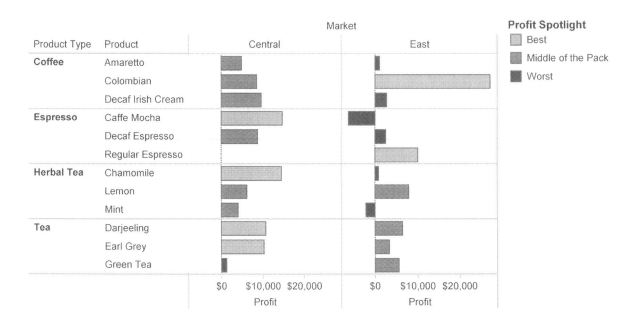

In this case, spotlighting makes it easy to see that Central has only one underperforming product, the products with the highest profits are different between Central and East, and East has many more underperforming products but also has the highest profit product.

! *Alternate Route:* This is a simple example that also can be done by using the Stepped Color function on the Edit Colors dialog. Editing the default color range can give the same effect with less effort than the calculation. Note that this alternate approach has less control over the exact cutoffs for color coding, so it is not always a better choice.

Add totals and subtotals

Totals and Subtotals give you the powerful ability to summarize your view at the view pane level (the crossing of categorical item values used in the view) or as a grand total or totals for rows and/or columns. Due to the nature of subtotals, they are available only if there are at least two dimensional items in either the Rows or Columns shelf.

Although the function includes the word "total", Tableau does not simply add up all the values—it uses the aggregation specified for the measures in your view. Therefore, totals for summed measures would be the sum of the sums in each cell, but the total for averaged measures would be the average of the underlying data values used in the cells.

Now, you are going to build upon the example from the previous section on spotlighting. **Duplicate the sheet by right-clicking on the worksheet tab and selecting Duplicate Sheet, open Show Me, change the view type to** *text tables* **and hide Show Me.** Exclude the Coffee and Tea product types from the view, **by clicking on Coffee, <Ctrl> and then Tea, then select Exclude in the balloon that pops up. From the Dimensions pane, add** *Market Size* **to the end of the Rows shelf. In the main menu, click on Analysis → Totals → Add All Subtotals.**

Add Subtotals to a spotlighted text table

Product Type / Product

Market	Market Size	Espresso				Herbal Tea			
		Caffe Mocha	Decaf Espresso	Regular Espresso	Total	Chamo..	Lemon	Mint	Total
Central	Major Market	$11,586	$6,211		$17,797	$6,576	$2,135	$4,069	$12,780
	Small Market	$3,056	$2,648		$5,704	$7,859	$4,118		$11,977
	Total	$14,642	$8,859		$23,501	$14,435	$6,253	$4,069	$24,757
East	Major Market	($6,069)	$1,738	$10,274	$5,943	$764	$6,955	($3,369)	$4,350
	Small Market	($163)	$673	($209)	$301		$947	$1,126	$2,073
	Total	($6,232)	$2,411	$10,065	$6,244	$764	$7,902	($2,243)	$6,423

Profit Spotlight

- Best
- Middle of the Pack
- Worst

Note that profits from all products and market sizes have been summed up in the table. However, grand totals are not shown, which would summarize across all markets or across all product types. Turn off Subtotals by **choosing Analysis → Totals → Remove All Subtotals on the main menu.** Turn on Grand Totals for both Rows and Columns: **Select Analysis → Totals → Show Row Grand Totals and Analysis → Totals → Show Column Grand Totals.**

Add Grand Totals to a spotlighted Text Table

| | | Product Type / Product | | | | | | |
| | | Espresso | | | Herbal Tea | | | |
Market	Market Size	Caffe Mocha	Decaf Espresso	Regular Espresso	Chamomi..	Lemon	Mint	Grand Total
Central	Major Market	$11,586	$6,211		$6,576	$2,135	$4,069	$30,577
	Small Market	$3,056	$2,648		$7,859	$4,118		$17,681
East	Major Market	($6,069)	$1,738	$10,274	$764	$6,955	($3,369)	$10,293
	Small Market	($163)	$673	($209)		$947	$1,126	$2,374
Grand Total		$8,410	$11,270	$10,065	$15,199	$14,155	$1,826	$60,925

Profit Spotlight
- Best
- Middle of the Pack
- Worst

In general, subtotals and grand totals are less useful when using bar or line chart views. Often, the totals greatly surpass the individual values, resetting the values on the axis labels and making the chart difficult to read. Totals often are more useful and easier to include on histograms, pie charts, and maps, or aggregations other than Sum and Count, such as Average, Minimum and Maximum.

Create a motion chart after connecting to a new data source

Motion charts were popularized by Hans Rosling, an eminent statistician and doctor specializing in public health, during a presentation he gave at a TED conference, a global organization that focuses on innovative ideas. He discussed the lifespans and health of people across many countries and how that has changed over time with societal and medical care advancements. A motion chart is great for this type of dataset—it is a simple yet powerful display that shows how the relationship of two measures (e.g., sales and profitability) changes over time. Usually, a category is divided into its members (e.g., the product line category is split into coffee, espresso, and tea).

Using marketing data for a boutique winery, you will create a standard motion chart in Tableau, which is a scatter plot combined with features of the Pages shelf. Note that the concept is also applicable to other chart types. In this case, the marketing manager of the winery is asking: "How does the relationship between customer segment and preferred marketing channel vary over time?"

If you have not already, **download and save the *Winery sales and customers* data from the Freakalytics web site at** http://www.Freakalytics.com/rgts8 Once downloaded, you'll connect to a new local data source.

On the main menu, **click Data → Connect to Data → In a file → Microsoft Excel. Find the Winery sales and customers data, click on it to select and press Open.** The Excel Workbook Connection dialog appears. Step 1 displays the file that you chose. The worksheet names appear in *Step 2: Select the worksheet (table) area to analyze.* **Select Sales data. Keep the default values for Steps 3 and 4 and click OK.**

Excel Workbook Connection dialog

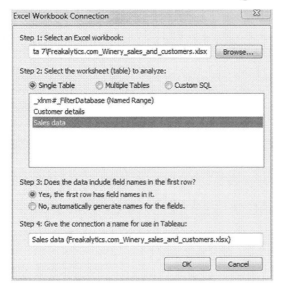

The Data Connection dialog appears with three choices: *Connect live* (connects directly to your data, *Import all data* (imports entire data source as a Tableau Data Extract) or *Import some data* (imports a subset of your data as a Tableau Data Extract).

The Data Connection dialog

Select the first choice—**Connect live.** You are now connected to your data! **Then you can save this work as a predefined data connection by right-clicking on it in the Data pane and choosing Add to Saved Data Sources.**

For simplicity, the method to build a motion chart is broken down into four steps.

Step 1. **Open the Winery customer and sales dataset. Select** *Customer Segment*, *Email Sales* **and** *Tasting Room Sales*. **Unhide Show Me, accept the default chart type,** *scatter plots*, **and hide Show Me**. **Change the aggregate for both metrics in the view from SUM to AVG. Additionally, format both data items as Currency.**

Step 1. The foundation for the motion chart

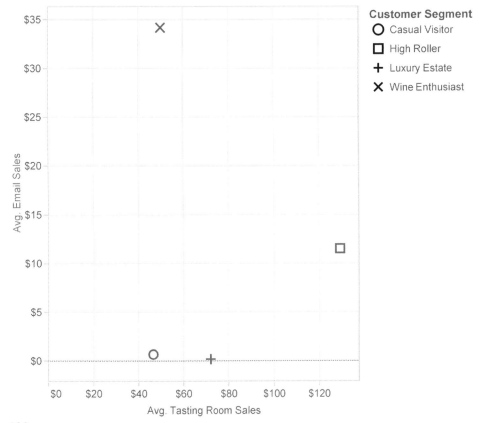

Step 2. Customer Segment is now on the Shape button on the Marks card—verify this by looking at the oval underneath the buttons. **Drag the** *Customer Segment* **oval to the Label button. On the dropdown on the Marks card, change the mark type from Automatic to Text. The Label button turns into the Text button. <Ctrl> + click and hold on the** *Customer Segment* **oval, then drag it to the Color button** (in Tableau, <Ctrl> + click creates a copy of any item in an oval so you can place it on another shelf or button).

! *Performance Tip*: If you have about 6-8 data points or less, you may want to label the data points with their names spelled out in text to make the final motion chart easier to follow.

Step 2. Prior to setting the chart in motion

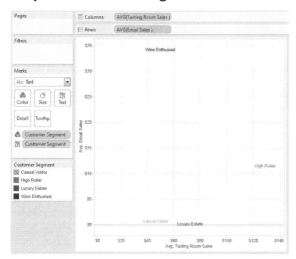

The Wine Enthusiast group responds very strongly to Email marketing, as the average spend is much higher than the other groups, but the High Rollers spend more during Tasting Room visits. Although this is useful information, now the marketing manager is curious about how this relationship has changed over time. This is where the motion chart becomes priceless (and perhaps entertaining)!

Step 3. Add *Date* **to the Pages shelf twice.** It will automatically switch to the *Year* and *Quarter* level of detail and now appears in the Pages Control with an initial value of ***2008, Q3***.

Step 3. Initial motion chart view

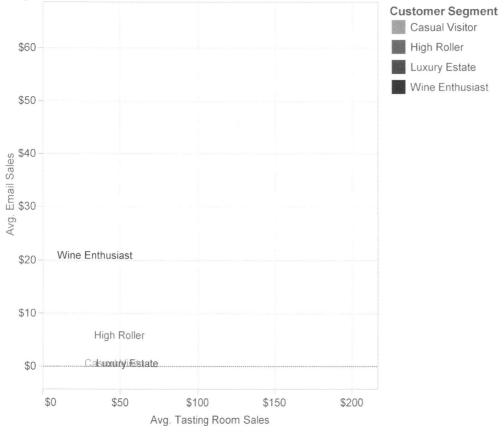

Unlike the Filters shelf, when you place items on the Pages shelf, Tableau incorporates the full range of values into the view for each item in the Pages dropdown. Using the range of possible outcomes, Tableau scales the axes of your plot accordingly. Notice that the range of values is quite different from the earlier view, and that the values are much lower for the segments that were leading earlier.

Step 4. **On the Pages control panel, click the checkbox for *Show History*.** The views look the same as before if you page through the different quarters in the graph. However, if you first click on one of the segments in the graph, the default history behavior turns on. It may be helpful to make this feature stand out more. **On the Pages control panel, turn on the *Trail* option by clicking the drop-down caret next to *Show History* and selecting Trails and then click on the caret again to close the menu. Page through the views, and then click on a segment to bring up the trails.** The example shows the trails over 8 quarters for the top 2 segments (to select both of them, use the <Ctrl> key directly in the view). Note that you can select the desired segment at any point and the trails will track the previous history, so you do not have to select it before placing it on the shelf.

Step 4. Example of motion chart with trails for selected items

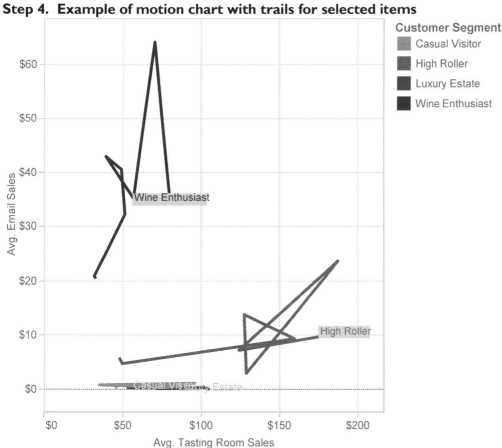

! *Performance Tip*: There is a wide array of additional options available with the ***Show History*** feature. Try them out!

The motion chart makes it easy to see the long-term direction of these two customer segments. For the High Rollers, the typical quarterly tasting room sales amount increased considerably, growing by nearly 400% in two years. E-mail sales remained relatively flat, at around 100% growth. The marketing manager may be particularly interested to see that e-mail sales spiked in Q4 of 2009 (up 400% from baseline, but only in a single quarter), yet rapidly returned to their earlier growth trajectory. It is probably a good idea for him to review e-mails from that quarter to figure out the messaging that works with this segment.

Meanwhile, the Wine Enthusiast segment has grown in both tasting room and e-mail sales over the past two years, with a possibly important drop in e-mail sales for the current quarter versus their earlier trajectory. Overall, Wine Enthusiasts are up about 60% to 300% in e-mail sales (depending on whether the last quarter was just an anomaly or the direction of future sales) and a solid 150% in tasting room sales.

Chapter 8

Essential Calculations and Models—
Quick Calculations, Custom Table Calculations,
Reference Lines, Trend Lines and Forecasting

Chapter Highlights

- Quick table calculations—complex calculations made easy

- Custom table calculations—the power to calculate specific metrics

- Reference lines, bands and distributions—emphasize useful values

- Trend Lines—model your data

- Forecasting—good starting point for building business plans

---

Now that you have experience in creating views, altering their appearance, and organizing them in useful ways, you are ready to move on to more complex manipulations of your view. This chapter will help you to answer advanced questions relatively quickly by optimizing the information displayed in your views. You will walk through examples of quick calculations where most of the work is done for you, custom table calculations that give you a lot of power to write complicated formulas, reference lines that help you to quickly review your data, trend lines that summarize overall data patterns, including some basic information about their interpretations and limitations, and forecast future possibilities based upon historical data. The goal is to give you an idea of the capabilities of Tableau, so that you are able to use them as a starting place for problems unique to your business.

You will be using two datasets: **Sample—Coffee Chain (Access)** provided by Tableau and *Winery customers and sales,* which you may have downloaded and used in the last chapter. If not, **download and save it from the Freakalytics website at** http://www.Freakalytics.com/rgts8 .

Quick Table Calculations

Quick Table Calculations are often related to date views and are applied to measures used in the view. Quick Table Calculations include:

- *Running Total* (versus prior period or cell)
- *Difference* (versus prior period or cell)
- *Percent Difference* (versus prior period or cell)
- *Percent of Total*
- *Moving Average* (smooth's out data that varies widely by time period)
- *Year-to-Date Total* (called YTD Total in Tableau)
- *Compound Growth Rate*
- *Year-over-Year Growth*
- *Year-to-Date Growth* (called YTD Growth in Tableau, and defined as cumulative YTD growth in measure over prior year).

The example shown can be created by **selecting** *Date* **and** *Profit* **from the Coffee Chain dataset. Open Show Me, select the default selection—*lines (discrete)*, and hide Show Me. Drill-down on the** *Date* **variable twice, from** *Year* **to** *Quarter* **and from** *Quarter* **to** *Month*. **This can be done by clicking on the plus sign located on the left side of the** *Date* **item oval on the Columns shelf.**

From the Data pane, add *Profit* **a second time to the Rows shelf and then add** *Sales* **to the Rows shelf. For the second** *Profit* **item on the Rows shelf, click on the down caret and select Quick Table Calculation → YTD Total. For** *Sales* **on the Rows shelf, click on the down caret and select Quick Table Calculation → YTD Total. Drag the** *Year(Date)* **item from the Columns shelf to the Color button on the Marks card.**

Quick Table Calculations—YTD Totals for *Profit* and *Sales*
Year in color

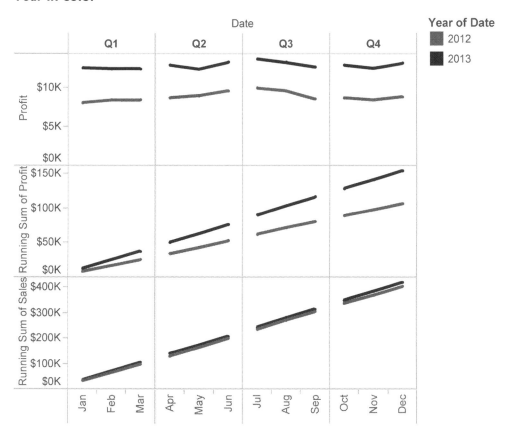

The Running Sums of *Profit* and *Sales* contrast quite dramatically. You can immediately observe very little difference in 2012 and 2013 sales growth through the year but substantially greater profit growth in 2013 over 2012. YTD running totals can help with estimating final sales and profit figures based on prior year patterns and current year trajectory. **Please save this worksheet as Quick Table, because you will return to it for the next two examples.**

Custom Table Calculations using data in your views

Quick Table Calculations are fast, convenient and very helpful. However, if you are used to writing complex formulas in Excel, they may not get the whole job done. For that reason, Tableau gives you the power to go well beyond default table calculations.

As you saw in the last example, table calculations allow easy comparison between the year-to-date sales and year-to-date profit. **For this example, duplicate the sheet from the last section (Quick Table) by right-clicking on the bottom tab and selecting Duplicate Sheet. Then delete all the measures (green ovals) except for Running Sum of Profit, which is the second** *SUM(Profit)* **on the Rows shelf.**

You can perform secondary table calculations on two types of table calculations: *running totals* and *moving calculations* (e.g., YTD Totals and Moving Averages). One common secondary calculation is to determine the percent difference from the prior year for running totals. For example, if the YTD was $75,787 in June 2013, and the YTD was $51,963 in June 2012, the YTD % growth was 45.8%. To add this to the example as a label above the lines, **<Ctrl> + click and hold on the** *SUM(Profit)* **data item on the Rows shelf and drag it to the Label button on the Marks card** This will duplicate the item so it is now on the Rows shelf and Label button. You will now see the YTD running total values on both lines (not shown).

On the bottom of the Marks card, hover over the SUM(Profit) oval, click on the drop-down caret and select Edit Table Calculation. The Table Calculation dialog appears. **Check** *Perform a secondary calculation on the result* and the dialog will expand. **Change the** *Secondary Type* **to "Percent Difference From", change** *Calculate the difference along* **to "Date" and** *At the level* **to "Year of Date".** The dialog should appear like the example below. **Click OK.**

The Table Calculation dialog with secondary calculation

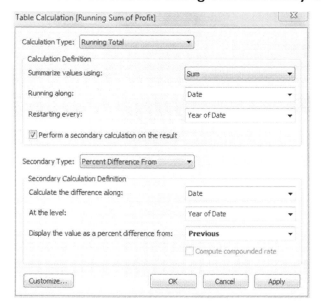

Secondary calculation determining the
percent difference from the prior year for running totals

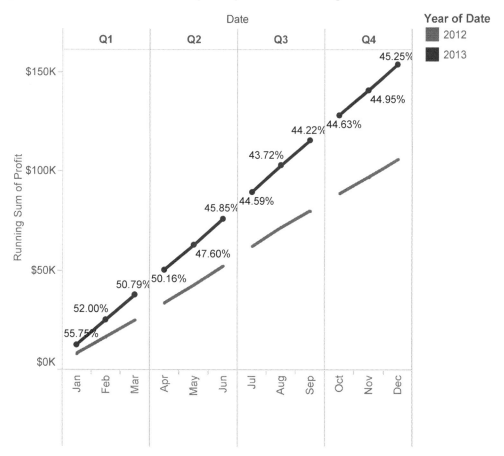

Here is a more advanced example. You want to view the running ratio of YTD profit over YTD sales (the YTD gross profit margin). You can create advanced table calculations using the Calculated Field dialog.

For this example, duplicate the sheet from the Quick Table section using the bottom tab. For *SUM(Sales)* **on the Rows shelf, click on the down caret and select Edit Table Calculation.** The Table Calculation dialog appears. **Click the Customize button and the Calculated Field dialog will appear.** It shows the formula used by Tableau to show YTD sales, **RUNNING_SUM(SUM([Sales])).**

To calculate YTD gross profit margin, enter this formula:
RUNNING_SUM(SUM([Profit])) / RUNNING_SUM(SUM([Sales]))
and change the Name to YTD Gross Margin. Click OK twice. YTD Gross Margin now appears in the third row of the view.

Advanced table calculations using the Calculated Field dialog

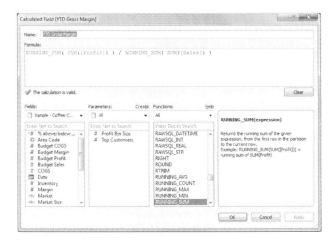

! *Performance Tip:* **If you click the Functions drop-down and change it from All to Table Calculation, you will see all of the available functions.** With a bit of imagination and practice, there is a huge array of possibilities once you understand these functions!

Advanced table calculations:
Profit, **YTD** *Profit* and **YTD** *Gross Margin*

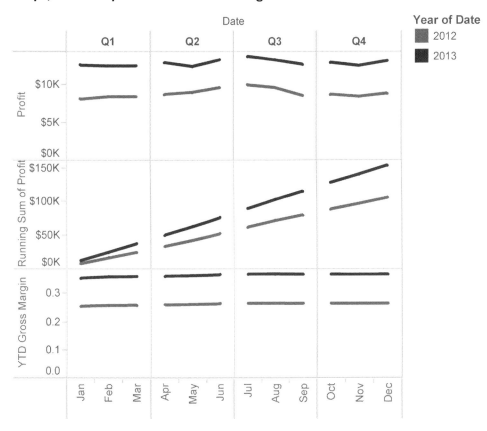

Now you are ready for an extremely advanced example of custom Table Calculations. **Open a new worksheet.** The next figure shows the average sales amount by state within each product of the Coffee Chain. The custom Table Calculation is used to show the percent difference in average sales for each state relative to the average state in each product. This value, *% above/below average order amount*, is used on the Color button and on the Label button. **To create this field on the main menu, go to Analysis →** **Create Calculated Field, and enter:**

(AVG([Sales]) - WINDOW_AVG(AVG([Sales])))
/
WINDOW_AVG(AVG([Sales]))

! *Performance Tip***:** Try to use the Fields and Functions selectors as much as possible to avoid typos in your formulas.

Type the title and click OK. Place *Product* **on the Columns shelf. Place** *Sales* **on the Rows shelf, and change to average. Place** *% above/below average order amount* **on the Color button and the Label button. Press the Label button, keep** *Show mark labels* **checked, and under Marks to Label, select Min/Max so labels will be shown only for the states with minimum and maximum values, and choose Cell for the Scope. Back on the Marks Card, change Automatic to Shape, and then add** *State* **to the Shape button (**if the warning appears, **accept it by selecting "Add all members").** **Press the Shape button and assign the open circle to every state except for Iowa, and then assign a filled-in diamond to Iowa. Turn on highlighting using the highlight button on the toolbar by** *State* **and select Iowa from the Shape legend. Sort by** *Product***, choosing Descending,** *Field* **→ Sales and then** *Aggregation* **→ Average.** This will give you the basic view—the one depicted below has more clean-up steps.

Average Sales Amount by *State* within each *Product*
of the **Coffee Chain**, with percent above/below average
order amount on **Label** and **Color** buttons

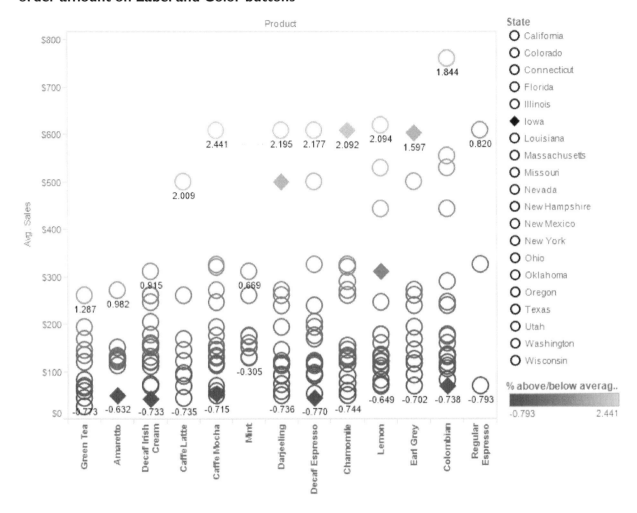

It is very interesting to see that Iowa has extreme product order variability. It is the top state in two of the nine products sold in the state, yet it is also the bottom state for five of the nine products. This would definitely be an interesting topic for product or regional managers to investigate.

If you create this view and see different values, you should verify that Tableau is calculating the *% above/below average order amount* using *State*. This is the NOT the default behavior for table calculations, which is to use Table (Across) as the direction of computation. **To correct this, use the dropdown menus on the data item ovals that are placed on the Label and Color buttons.**

Dropdown menu for the data item oval on the Color button

Change default direction of computation

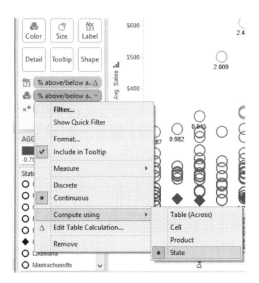

One final example of the power of custom table calculations to enhance your views is using the INDEX function. This returns the "row" number of an item based on the sorting used in your view. This example reinforces the importance of using the right sort order and Compute using item.

If you have not already used the Winery dataset, **download and save the *Winery sales and customers* data from the Freakalytics web site at** http://www.Freakalytics.com/rgts8

On the main menu, **click Data → Connect to Data → In a file → Microsoft Excel. Find the Winery sales and customers data, click on it to select and press Open.** The Excel Workbook Connection dialog appears. Step 1 displays the file that you chose. The worksheet names appear in *Step 2: Select the worksheet (table) area to analyze*. **Select Sales data. Keep the default values for Steps 3 and 4 and click OK.**

The Data Connection dialog appears with three choices: **Select the first choice—*Connect live*.** You are now connected to your data! **Then you can save this work as a predefined data connection by right-clicking on it in the Data pane and choosing Add to Saved Data Sources.**

Now you are going to create a map of total newsletter sales (SUM) by state. **Double-click** *State* **and then double-click** *Sale Amount*. To zoom in on the map, **highlight the data points in the continental U.S., and in the tooltip that appears when you hover, select Keep Only. Next, use the main menu, Analysis → Create Calculated Field, to create a new calculated field named RANK with the very simple Formula: INDEX( ) . Place the new item RANK on the Label button.** Notice that all states appear to be ranked as "1", but clearly, this is incorrect.

Click the drop down for the RANK item oval that is on the Label button and change the *Compute using* **value from Table (Across) to** *State (Abbr)*. Now, each state shows a unique value for rank, but it appears that the ranking is not by *Newsletter Sales* but rather by the alphabetic order of the state names (e.g., Washington is 46 even though it is the top state for *Newsletter Sales*). To fix this last issue, **click the drop down for the** *State* **oval that is on the Detail button, select Sort and set the sort to be Descending by** *Field* *Sale Amount* **using** *Aggregation* **Sum.**

Use the INDEX function for ranking data items in views

Remember to sort the data in the order of the ranking!

Reference Lines, Bands and Distributions

Reference lines, bands or distributions may be added to your views to emphasize particular values or areas that are useful in interpreting your data. In particular, when comparing multiple groups or categories of data, reference lines and bands provide immediate feedback on the overall differences between the groups.

Reference lines are vertical or horizontal lines displayed on your view that mark requested values such as average, median, minimum, maximum, sum, total and constants (such as a line that separates the data points as being above or below a target). They can be added on any continuous axis.

Create a new worksheet, <Ctrl> + M. Use the Coffee Chain data source. From the Data pane, drag *Sales* to the Columns shelf and change the aggregate to Average. From the Data pane, drag *Product* to the Rows shelf, change the mark type from Automatic to Shape on the Marks card, and press the Shape button to change the shape to a Plus sign. From the Data pane, drag *State* and *Date* to the Detail button.

The view currently shows one mark <u>per year</u>/state/product combination. For more detail, show one mark <u>per month</u>/year/state/product combination. **At the bottom of the Marks card, hover over the blue YEAR(Date) oval and click on the down caret that appears.** The drop-down menu appears for any date field that is placed on the Detail button, which allows quick selection of date data as either discrete (first date section) or continuous (second date section).

Select the continuous version of Month. After you make this change, notice that now the item is called *MONTH(Date)*, and instead of being colored as a discrete item (blue), it is a continuous item (green).

Right-click on the *Avg. Sales* axis. Choose Add Reference Line, change Scope to Per Cell, and click OK. Add a second reference line by opening the Add Reference Line dialog again and changing Scope to Per Cell and Average to Median and clicking OK. If you prefer, change the labels and colors of the reference lines by **right-clicking on the axis and selecting Edit Reference Line. Finally, sort the view in descending order by average sales amount.**

Reference lines for average (black) and median (gray)

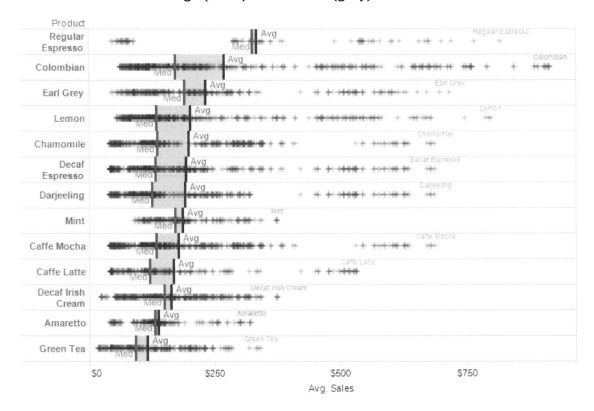

Reference bands are shaded areas, typically highlighting the range of values in a section of the view. They cover the area between two relevant values, such as average and median, or minimum and maximum, which are illustrated in the next example.

Duplicate the prior sheet and right-click on the *Avg. Sales* **axis to select Remove All Reference Lines. From the Data pane, drag** *Market* **to the Columns shelf to the left of** *Sales*. **Right-click on the** *Avg. Sales* **axis and select Add Reference Line, choose the Band icon at the top, Scope Per Cell, Band From Minimum to Maximum, and change both Labels to None. You also can format.**

Reference bands for range between minimum and maximum

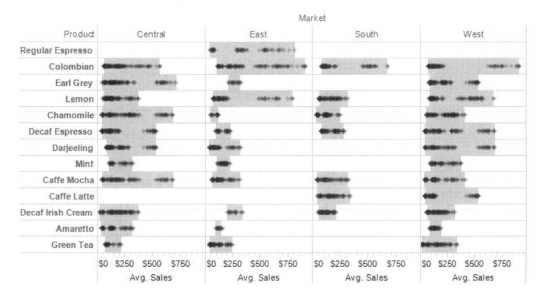

Reference distributions are a modification of reference bands—they typically shade areas above, below and between two requested statistics. The difference is that they represent a distribution of values along an axis, and include confidence intervals, percentages, percentiles, quantiles and standard deviation.

Duplicate the last sheet. Remove the reference line and *Market* **from the Columns shelf. Right-click on the** *Avg. Sales* **axis, select Add Reference Line, choose Distribution and Per Cell, and under Computation, choose Percentiles and type in 10,90. You also can change the formatting settings.**

Reference distribution for the 10th and 90th percentiles

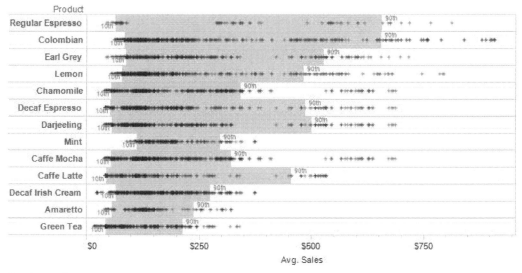

Tableau allows you to customize reference lines, bands and distributions in many different ways, so check out the menus to explore the wide array of options.

Model your data with Trend Lines

Tableau can model your data with a trend line to help you visualize the overall patterns of the data. The trend line can be based on a linear, logarithmic, exponential or polynomial regression model. Additionally, the trend can be adjusted across dimensional levels so that each pane has a fitted line for the data displayed in that pane. For Tableau to calculate a valid trend line, the data items that are on your horizontal and vertical axes need to be equally spaced or have the ability to be converted into a range of continuous values. This includes continuous dimension items, measures added as dimensions, and date dimension items.

Tableau can use trend lines to report significance levels between two variables based on a regression model. Since statistical significance is a complex topic, we will not describe it in detail. One simple way to explain significance is with a p-value, which indicates how well the model fits your data. Lower p-values are better, with values less than 0.05 typically considered "statistically significant", usually written as $p<0.05$.

For example, a p-value of 0.03 tells you that there is a 3% chance that the trend line fitting your data values is describing a relationship between your two variables that is random or does not actually exist (i.e., 3% chance that there is no true pattern and the relationship is only noise). Or stated another way, the probability is that three times out of one-hundred, the relationship described by the trend line doesn't actually exist, while ninety-seven times out of one-hundred, it probably does exist. In Tableau, p-values are available for the entire model, a particular line in a pane, and specific data items used to explain the relationship between your numeric variables.

For example, you may want to try to estimate profit from sales. **Use <Ctrl> + M to open a new worksheet. Add** *Profit* **to the Rows shelf.** Note that the item you want to "predict" should be on the vertical or Y-axis, which corresponds to the Rows shelf. **Next, add** *Sales* **to the Columns shelf.** To use all data points in the Trend Line model, turn off the aggregation of data by **de-selecting Analysis →
Aggregate Measures using the main menu. Reduce the size of the data points to the smallest setting by pressing the Size button on the Marks card and moving the slider to the far left.**

Scatter plot of *Profit* vs. *Sales*

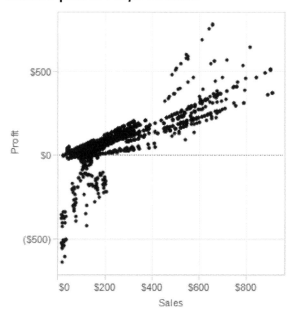

Add a trend line to the view by **right-clicking on the scatter plot and selecting Trend Lines → Show Trend Lines.** The trend line appears with the default linear (straight) form. To describe the fit of the trend line, **right-click on the scatter plot again and select Trend Lines → Describe Trend Model.** The Describe Trend Model dialog box appears (which you can copy to a clipboard).

Scatter plot of *Profit* vs. *Sales* with Trend Line

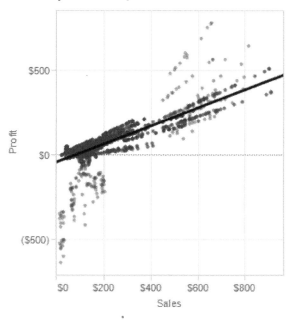

Describe Trend Model dialog box

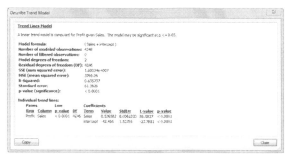

Note that the trend line appears to be drawn across the middle of the data points with some data point outliers towards the bottom left and upper right. There is a noticeable band of data points near the line, so the trend line is a good description of the data, but you can see that it does not perfectly fit the relationship between *Profit* and *Sales*. Note that the Describe Trend Model box shows a significant p-value of < 0.0001. It also shows another very valuable statistic called the R-Squared, which attempts to estimate how much of the data variability is actually explained by the model. In this case, 0.636, or 63.6% of the variability in the data values is accounted for by using *Sales* to predict *Profit*. At the bottom of the pane, you will find the values that can be used to estimate *Profit from Sales*: multiply *Sales* by 0.537 and subtract 42.5 to estimate *Profit* (you may remember this as the slope formula from your algebra days: y=mx+b or *Profit* = 0.537*Sales* − 42.5). This makes sense since you have fixed costs (the intercept, − 42.5) and variable costs (you make an additional 53.7 cents in profit for each additional dollar of sales)! Close the box.

To further refine the trend line, change the type of line fit. For example, draw trend lines based on year and market. **From the Data pane, drag *Date* to the Columns shelf before *Sales* and drag *Market* to the rows shelf before *Profit*. Finally, add *Product Type* to the Color button on the Marks card and keep only the Central region by right-clicking on it in the view and selecting Keep Only.** The Central region is chosen since it appears to have a very strong relationship between *Sales* and *Profit*, shown by the tight grouping of the data points around the trend lines. **Open the Describe Trend Model Box.**

Modify Trend Lines based on *Year* and *Market*

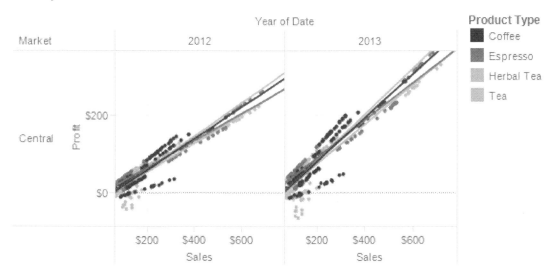

The p-value is still < 0.0001 (highly significant), but the large improvement in R-Squared from 0.638 to 0.891 is exciting. The model accounts for almost all (89.1%) of the variability in actual profit versus expected profit! In real-world business applications, it is rare to see R-Squared values above 60-80%, so this is very impressive. Examining the other fields used in the model, you can see that both *Product Type* and *Year of Date* are significant factors in explaining the model. Each *Product Type* has its own trend line and therefore a unique model describing the relationship between *Profit* and *Sales* for that *Product Type* only.

If you wanted to experiment further with the line type or other aspects of the model, **right-click on the graph and select Trend Lines → Edit Trend Lines.** The Trend Lines Options dialog box appears. Here you can change the model type and factors included in the model. You can choose to allow a trend line per color (in this case automatically selected) instead of one trend line overall for all of the colors, or product types in this example. You also can force the y-intercept to zero.

Trend Lines Options dialog box

Research modeling in a statistical textbook if you need in-depth information about the topic, although we summarize important points to consider about trend line models and statistical analysis:

1) A model with a good fit does not necessarily imply that one variable causes changes to occur in the second variable. For example, a statistically significant model relating temperature with rainfall does not demonstrate that one causes the other to fluctuate, just that the model can describe the relationship between the two. Further knowledge of the process at hand is required to assess if one variable causes changes in the other. The model simply shows they move together.

2) A statistically significant model, indicated by the p-value, can usually be created by adding enough data points. Be sure to examine the R-Squared to see how much of the variability in the data can be explained.

3) R-Squared can be skewed by adding more explanatory variables or factors to a trend line model, so try to use a reasonable number of factors to explain the relationship. In general, fewer items that have a high R-Squared are better than many items with a slightly higher R-Squared.

4) Be careful about using this type of model to forecast future values—especially if the external factors around your historic data have changed significantly!

5) If you have several factors in a model that are significant and you would like to remove some to simplify the model, first try removing the ones with the lower SSE values. SSE values measure how much of the data variability is explained by the factor, so factors with higher values for SSE are generally better to keep.

Forecasting

Forecasting is the process of planning for the future by estimating outcomes using statistical methods. For example, you could use a simple trend line to forecast future outcomes. This is a simplistic approach that has some appeal. In this example, future sales are estimated.

Forecasting future sales using simple trend line

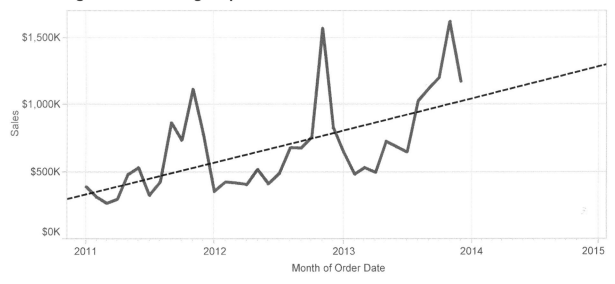

While this trend line appears to capture the general direction of sales at this company, if you examine the historical data you can see its limitations. In particular, it seems that there is a seasonal pattern, with some months having much higher sales than others. However, the trend line doesn't capture any of this information—it's simply a line.

Basically, the forecasting feature in Tableau uses advanced statistical methods to take in account seasonal patterns, age of data, and multiple possible models for predicting the future data and automatically picks the likely "best" model. The core of forecasting is a technique called exponential smoothing, in which more recent values are much more important in the forecast than older values.

Now, build a forecast model. **Open a new sheet in Tableau and select the Sample—Superstore—English (Extract). <CTRL> + Click on** *Order Date* **and** *Sales* **and select the default Show Me view type, lines (discrete). Right-click on the chart and select Forecast → Show Forecast. Filter on** *Order Date* **to use only 2011, 2012 and 2013 data. On the Columns shelf, drill down on** *YEAR(Order Date)* **to** *QUARTER(Order Date)*. **Click the dropdown on the Quarter item and change it to Month.**

Forecast for Sales in 2014, based on 2011, 2012 and 2013 data
Actual data are dark lines, *Estimate* (or forecast) is light line
Note that December 2013 is a light dot

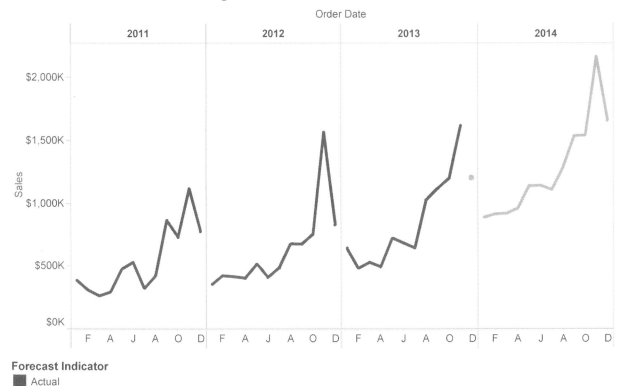

Forecast Indicator
■ Actual
■ Estimate

An arrow on the data item oval indicates that it is the target of the forecast, in this case, *SUM(Sales)*.

Forecasted data item indicated by an arrow

In this example, the forecasting feature detected both the seasonal pattern in the sales data (on an annual basis) and an annual upward trend. The estimated minimum for 2014 is in January and the estimated maximum is in November.

Notice that December 2013 has a light colored dot instead of a dark line, so this is a forecasted value (referred to as Estimate). However, the historic data (referred to as Actual) includes December 2013. Why is this displayed as a forecast? If December 2013 was a partial month (all of the sales data weren't in yet), then the forecast would be significantly affected because data were missing, decreasing the estimate or forecast due to the exponential smoothing technique. If this default assumption of Tableau is incorrect, to truncate the last period in your data due to the assumption that it is incomplete, change it with the Forecasting options dialog. **Right-click on the view and select Forecast → Forecast Options**. The Forecast Options dialog appears.

The Forecast Options dialog

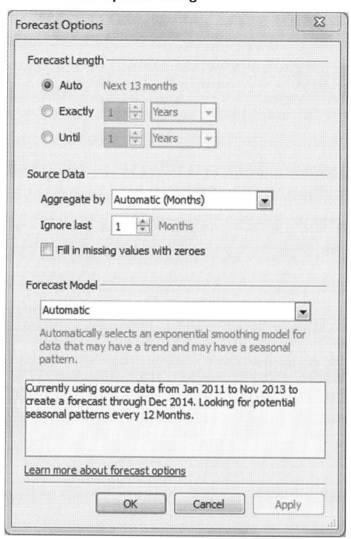

There are a wide range of options, including:

- How far into the future to forecast—note that to control the future values that are displayed, you must use this dialog (not the Filter dialog)
- What level of detail to forecast (month, week, quarter, etc.)
- Whether or not to ignore the last periods of the historic data and if so, how many periods
- The possibility to substitute missing values with zero values—a critical problem in some data; you may want to investigate various data interpolation methods
- Which forecast model to use—models include Automatic (default), Automatic without seasonality, Trend and season, Trend only, Season only and No trend or season

In this case, **change the Source Data → Ignore last option from 1 to 0. Click OK.** This completes the dark line for 2013.

Forecast with source data changed

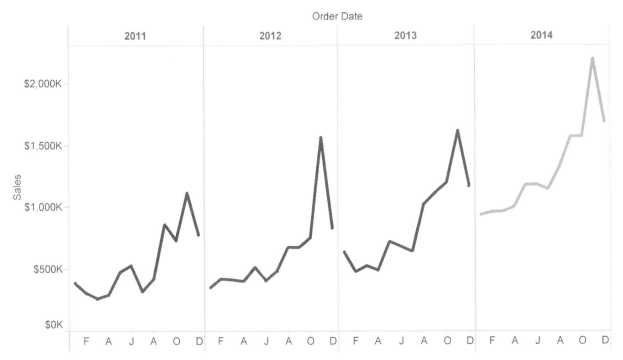

Next, on the Rows shelf, click on the dropdown for the forecasted data item.

Dropdown for forecasted data item, *SUM(Sales)*

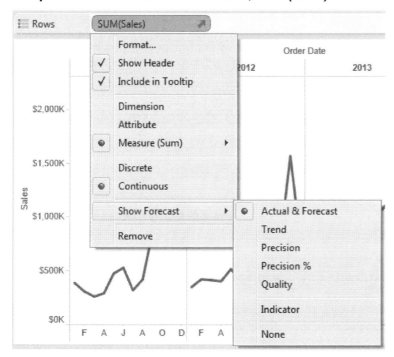

This menu includes the options for that data item. You can display the Trend (the forecast *without* seasonality), Precision and Precision % (how much to add or subtract from the displayed forecast for a statistically likely range of outcomes), and Quality and Indicator (whether it is actual data or estimated data.)

To obtain details about your forecast model, **right-click on the graph and select Forecast → Describe Forecast.** There are two tabs in this dialog.

The Describe Forecast dialog

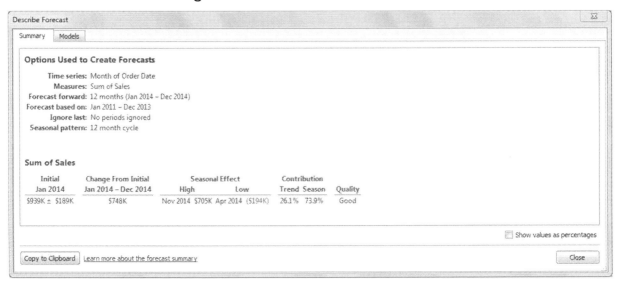

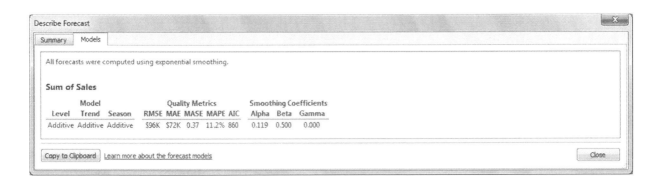

The first tab is a summary of the model built, assumptions selected, Initial forecast values, change from first to last forecast value, seasonal highs and lows, how much the trend and seasonality contributed to the model and whether the model quality is Good, Fair or Poor.

The second tab describes the models, including whether a Level was selected (starting overall height), a Trend was selected (angle up or down), a Season was selected (is there seasonality, otherwise the line will be straight) and various other model statistics that are underneath the model. Notably, the MASE statistic is the one used by Tableau to optimize the forecast model (a very smart developer, Scott, built this feature for Tableau 8).

For more possibilities with forecasting, visit http://www.Freakalytics.com/rgts8 and watch our videos on Better Analytics with Tableau 8. This video has an accompanying sample workbook so you can follow along at your own pace, if you like.

Chapter 9

Managing data is critical for great results— Data items and data management in Tableau

---

Chapter Highlights

- Data items

    o Names

    o Types

    o Roles

    o Properties

    o Geographic roles

    o Useful management functions

    o Custom data hierarchies

- View Data to see the data behind your view

- Bins to divide numeric data items

- Group dimensions into categories

- The power of sets to combine and filter your views

Data management no longer has to be intimidating and confusing—Tableau makes it easier for most people to manage their data with a wide array of simple yet powerful features. This chapter is quite important because effective data management is a frequently overlooked key to analytic success!

Please note that the examples in this chapter use the **Sample—Superstore—English (Extract)** data source, included with the Tableau application.

Data items: names, types, roles, properties, attributes and hierarchies

Data item names

Item names are based on the names in your selected data source. Within Tableau, you can rename items to make them relevant for your audience. For example, the item name "Profit" may seem reasonable for the Marketing team but might not be a specific enough name for the Finance team, who refer to this item as "Gross Profit". Note that renaming an item has no effect on the names in the original data source.

From the Measures pane, right-click on *Profit* **and select Rename from the menu.** The Rename Field dialog appears—**change the name to** *Gross Profit* **and click OK.**

Rename Field dialog box (Field refers to your data item)

If you think an item may be irrelevant or confusing, it can be hidden from view by **right-clicking on the item and selecting Hide.** To return hidden items to the view, **click on the down caret next to Dimensions in the Data Items pane, and select Show Hidden Fields.**

Data item types

Tableau offers five types of data items: **Number**, **Date & time**, **Date**, **String and Boolean**. By default, when Tableau connects to your data, it determines which type is the best match for a data item using the data source information and rules around data types. It is important to note that items will behave differently in your views based on the data type. Typically, you only will need to modify data types when using Access, Excel or text files as data sources. Relational and multi-dimensional databases are usually pre-formatted so that Tableau can select the correct data types when you open them.

It is easy to change data types from the item context menu by **right-clicking on the item and selecting Change Data Type.** These are the rules for changing data types:

- Any data type can be converted to _String_.
- A _Number_ can be converted to _Date_ or _Date & time_, but this should only be done if the number values meet date convention requirements for your data source.
- _Date_ and _Date & time_ can be easily interchanged:
  - Dates simply add 00:00:00 as the time when converted to _Date & time_.
  - _Date & time_ fields lose their time aspect if converted to _Date_.

To change the default type, **from the Dimensions pane, right-click on Order ID, select Change Data Type → String.**

The Change Data Type submenu

Data item roles: dimensions and measures

In Tableau, **dimensions** and **measures** are the primary means of grouping data items in the Data Items pane. By default, Tableau treats any field containing qualitative (e.g., customer type of "New", "Old", "Returning") or categorical (e.g., region of "West", "East") information as a *dimension*. In general, *dimensions* are items used to create row or column headers in a view.

By default, Tableau treats any field containing numeric information as a *measure*. *Measures* typically produce axes when added to the rows or columns shelves. *Measures* are computed using the specified aggregation for each unique combination of row and column *dimensions* used in the view. For example, if the measure is **Sales**, the data source engine calculates **SUM(Sales)** for each dimension item combination (e.g., State and Month) used in the view.

There is an important technical detail to add to this explanation of dimensions and measures. Tableau does not scan the values in your data items, which could be slow and inefficient. Instead, it uses the metadata provided by your data source, which is a description about your data, to identify and organize your dimensions and measures.

You can convert *measures* to *dimensions* and *dimensions* to *measures*, although more often you will convert *measures* to *dimensions* due to Tableau defaults. You can convert an item from *measure* to *dimension* **by dragging it from the Measures pane to the Dimensions pane, or you can right-click on it and select Convert to Dimension.** You also can perform this action on an item placed on a shelf if you need to convert the item only for that particular view.

For example, you may want to use *Discount* as a *dimension* so you can view all values separately rather than creating an axis from this field. In the following example, **the first view, the scatter plot, is the default Show Me view for** *Discount (Measure)*, *Profit* **and** *Region* (*Region* **was moved from the shape button to the color button) with the** *International* **region excluded. The second view, the bar chart, is the default Show Me view for** *Discount (Dimension)*, *Profit* **and** *Region* **(with** *Region* **copied onto the Color button and** *International* **region excluded), after swapping Columns and Rows.**

Default Show Me views: *Discount* **(Measure) versus** *Discount* **(Dimension)**

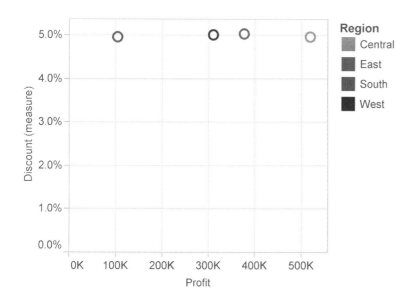

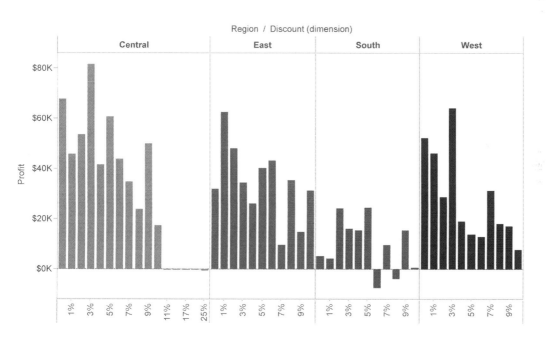

Notice that the level of detail regarding *Discount* increases after it is converted to a *dimension*. As a measure, one value for each region is displayed—the average discount for that region. As a dimension, all of the unique values used in each region are shown.

It may be helpful to know that if the change is required only for the current view, **use the down caret next to the item on the Columns or Rows shelf to select Dimension. Alternatively, copy the item into the Dimensions pane, and you will have both forms of the data item for future use.**

Data item roles: continuous versus discrete data items

In Tableau, all data items are classified as either **continuous** or **discrete**. In the Data Items pane, the icons located to the left of all data items are color-coded as green (*continuous*) or blue (*discrete*). Additionally, when you select a particular data item, *discrete* items will be framed with a blue oval and *continuous* items by a green one. When added to the Rows or Columns shelves, *continuous* items always create axes and *discrete* items always create headers.

You can convert both measures and dimensions that are *continuous* items to *discrete* and *discrete* items to *continuous*, although more often you will convert *continuous* to *discrete* due to the Tableau defaults. **Do this by right-clicking on the item in the Data Items pane and selecting Convert to Discrete. In addition, moving a data item from the Measures pane to the Dimensions pane** will switch it from continuous to discrete (unless it already was discrete). **If the change is required only for the current view, use the down caret next to the item on the Columns or Rows shelf to select Discrete.**

In a new worksheet, continue from the last example by **converting** Discount **from *discrete* to *continuous* in the Dimensions pane. For** Discount (Continuous Dimension) **and** Profit **(with** Department **on the Color button) select a continuous lines chart from the Show Me menu. Create a new worksheet and then convert** Discount **back to *discrete*. Choose the default Show Me view, *horizontal bars*, for** Discount (Discrete Dimension) **and** Profit. **When you place** Department **on the Color button, the view will change to stacked bars.**

Discount (Continuous Dimension) versus *Discount* (Discrete Dimension)

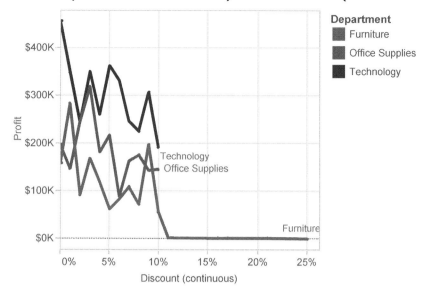

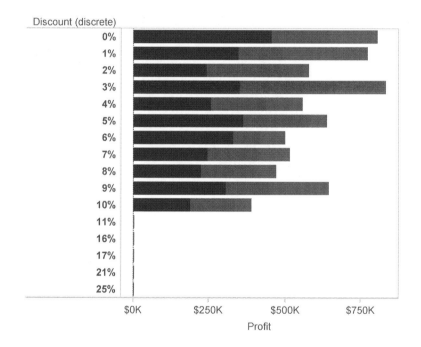

Notice the very different representation of *Discount* as a *continuous* item versus a *discrete* item. The *continuous* graph has no gaps between the discount values, so it displays the long tail at the end for *Furniture* (from 11% to 25%) better than the *discrete* graph, which has separate marks for 11, 16, 17, 21 and 25%.

How various types of data items behave in Tableau depending upon the combination, such as *discrete measure* or *continuous dimension*, can be quite complicated. When discussing how to approach this topic, we quickly wound up in a parody of *Who's on First* ("Is Discount a continuous measure?" "No, I turned it into a discrete dimension…"). Experiment to see how different data items appear in multiple views!

Data item properties

All data items have default field properties that can be customized. You can customize them while they are still in the Data Items pane or after you add them to the view. Although there are special field properties for particular types of data items, there are five main ones for most dimensions, **Comment, Aliases, Color, Shape and Sort** and four for most measures, **Comment, Color, Number Format,** and **Aggregation.**

Default properties for dimensions:

- **Comment**—any concise information that you would like to include about the data item, for yourself or others. For example, for Product Category, you may note, "categories were renamed in 2011".
- **Alias**—how the text or labels are displayed, for example changing "NE" to display as "Northeast". Note that dates and continuous dimensions have no aliases since the actual values must be displayed.
- **Color**—affects the default color for values, such as "Exceeds plan" displayed as green and "Below plan" displayed as red.
- **Shape**—the default shape for a value, such as a filled green circle means "Exceeds plan" and a filled red diamond means "Below plan". Note that only a few shapes have intrinsic color like these special KPI (Key Performance Indicators) shapes. Most shapes use the colors automatically specified for them by the Color button.
- **Sort**—establishes a default sort order, for instance, manually select the sort order for 'State'. Note that the sorting options are limited versus the Row or Column shelves.

Default properties for measures:

- **Comment**—similar to comments for dimensions, these are notes about the data item that you think are important.
- **Color**—similar to color for dimensions, this affects the default color values. An example is coloring marks representing profit red for loss and green for gain.
- **Number Format**—allows you to choose number formatting, such as currency or percentage. Some dimensional items, such as Date, also can be formatted.
- **Aggregations**—such as sum or average are available, except for geographic locations.

To modify the field properties from the Data Items pane, **right-click on the item, select Default Properties and pick the property that you wish to edit.** However, changing properties of a data item on either the shelves or in the view will override those properties. The next several figures are examples of what you can do if you adjust field properties in various ways.

"Audience-friendly" aliases for *Order Priority*—default versus customized

Appropriate colors for *Order Priority*—default versus customized

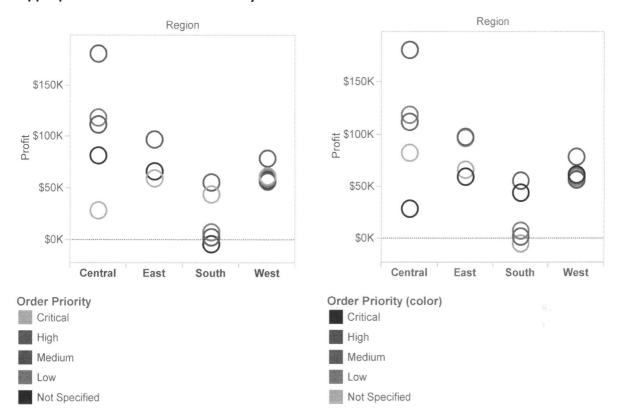

Order Priority
- Critical
- High
- Medium
- Low
- Not Specified

Order Priority (color)
- Critical
- High
- Medium
- Low
- Not Specified

Shape for *Order Priority* changed to corporate standards

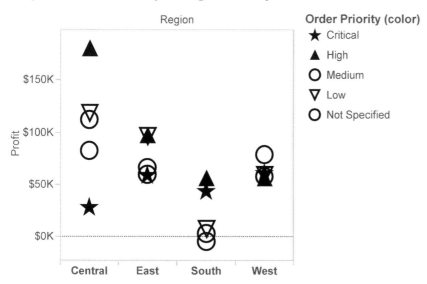

Order Priority (color)
- ★ Critical
- ▲ High
- ○ Medium
- ▽ Low
- ○ Not Specified

Sort order of *Profit*—default versus manual

Number format of *Shipping Cost* relative to *Sales*— default (profit ratio) versus formatted (percent)

Aggregation of *Profit*—default *sum* versus *average*

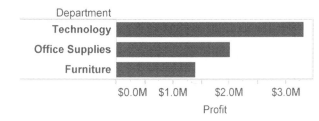

To create this last example, **turn off Aggregate Measures from the Analysis menu to display all records on view. Filter data for top three customers by Sum of Sales.** Note that all profit records for these top three customers are shown individually versus the aggregated bar chart views above.

Go beyond default roles with no aggregation

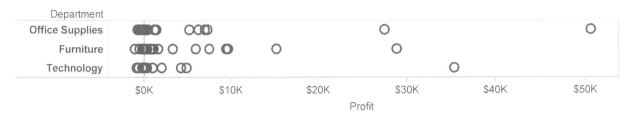

Data items: geographic roles

Tableau offers exciting mapping capabilities to overlay your data onto relevant maps. By default, Tableau automatically assigns a geographic role to data items that have certain name and data types assigned to them.

Geographic Role	Description
Area Code	U.S. 3-digit area code
CBSA / MSA	U.S. Core Based Statistical Area e.g., Dallas-Fort Worth-Arlington
City	U.S. and worldwide with at least 15,000 residents
Congressional District	U.S. only State-provided data on boundaries of areas
Country / Region	Name → English, German and French ISO 3166-2 → 2-character abbreviation ISO 3166-3 → 3-character abbreviation FIPS 10 code → standard officially ended in 2008
County	U.S. county names
Latitude / Longitude	If available in dataset, can use instead of Tableau's geocoding
State / Province	Name → English, German and French U.S. States & Worldwide Abbreviation → Only available in certain countries such the U.S., the U.K. and Canada
Zip Code / Postcode	U.S. 5-digit zip code Postal codes for France, Germany, U.K., Australia, New Zealand and Canada

All other items have a default geographic role of **None**. Additionally, you can add your own geographic roles to extend the capabilities of Tableau, such as the location of your stores based on store identifier or all the airports in the world based on their three letter code.

If Tableau does not properly identify your geographic item, you can change this role by **right-clicking on the item, selecting Geographic Role and choosing the proper geographic role from the above**

list. Once your data item is assigned a geographic role, it is distinguished with a small globe icon. Your dataset may have some miscoded items that Tableau cannot map.

Open the Winery customer and sales dataset once again, choosing the Sales data table. Select *Zip Code* **and** *E-mail Sales*. **Unhide Show Me, accept the default chart type,** *symbol maps*, **and hide Show Me**. On the Marks card, change **the aggregate from SUM to AVG. Add** *State* **to the Filter shelf and exclude AK, HI and PR.** The zooms the view in on the map. Notice that there is a message at the bottom right of your map: "15 unknown". This is a warning that 15 zip codes cannot be mapped.

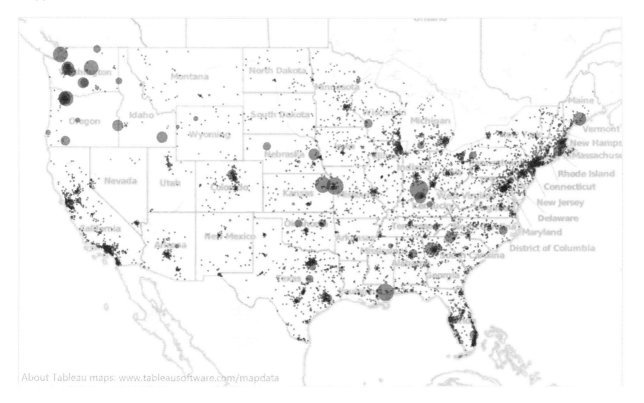

There are three ways to correct the unknown Zip Codes by selecting Edit Locations: go to Map on the main menu, right-click on the map itself, or click on the gray warning box in the lower right. Click on the gray warning box and the Special Values dialog appears.

Special Values dialog

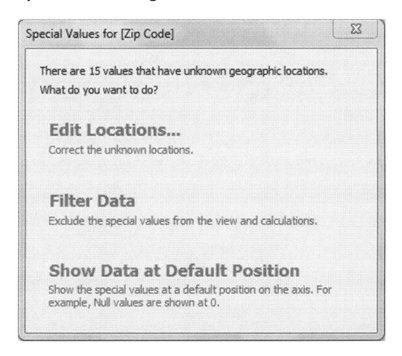

Note that you can also filter the unknown values and remove them from the view or map them at a default location. **Click on Edit locations.** The Geographic Roles submenu appears so you can recode these items to their proper values. See the following example demonstrating this with Zip Code data, which Tableau requires to be five digits in length.

Recoding unmatched location data

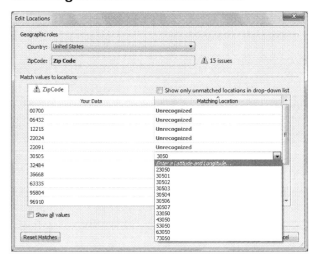

Data items: useful management functions

Other simple data management utilities available from a data item's right-click menu include:

Replace References: this very powerful command will replace all reference to the selected item in your Tableau Workbook with another item. *Be careful, this includes the use of the item in every sheet and in calculated items!* Of course, your views will reflect this change immediately.

Describe: this command will give you very detailed information about the item including role, type, default aggregation, comment, status (is it valid or not?), the formula used for the item and the domain of the item. The domain is a list of values or a range of values. **You must click Load** to see the domain, so do not do this for very large lists of distinct values!

The Describe Field dialog—data item details

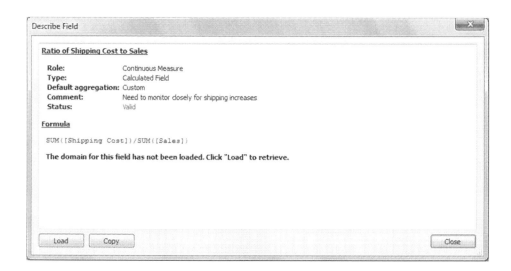

Duplicate: this command will perform an equivalent of copy and paste all at once. You will see a duplicate version of the item copied with a new suffix on the item name. Typically, "(copy)" is appended to the original item name. Note that this does not modify your original data source; it merely creates a new item referencing it. This command is useful when you need to reuse a calculated field formula or simultaneously require the same item as a dimension and a measure.

Rename: this command allows you to rename an item with a name more relevant for your workbook.

Hide: irrelevant or potentially confusing items can be hidden from users of your workbook with this command. No changes are made to your original data source when you use this command; the item simply is not displayed in your Data Items pane. Hiding also removes the item from *View Data* and prevents it from being extracted. Note that you cannot hide a data item that is being used in a view or formula in the worksheet.

Unhide: To unhide items, **click on the dropdown menu at the upper right of the Dimensions pane and select "Show Hidden Fields".** The hidden fields will appear in the pane as grayed-out items. **You must right-click on the item and select unhide for it to be available for use in your workbook.**

Hide All Unused Fields: this command will hide all fields not currently in use in the workbook. This is very useful for simplifying the Data Items pane list of large data sources. To hide all unused items, **click on the dropdown menu at the upper right of the Dimensions pane and select "Hide All Unused Fields"**.

Show Hidden Fields: once you have hidden fields, this option becomes available. Just because you have shown the hidden fields, which appear as light gray data items, does not mean you can use them in views. **You must first right-click on the desired items and select Unhide**.

Sort Data Items: the data items in the Dimensions and Measures panes are sorted alphabetically by their names by default. If you would prefer to see them ordered by their original data source order, **click on the dropdown menu at the upper right of the Dimensions pane and select Sort By → Data Source Order**. This is very useful for very wide tables that have the items in a particular order.

The "Sort by" option in the Data Items pane

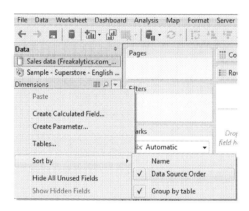

Delete: this command is available only for calculated fields. All other fields can be hidden. The main difference is that once a calculated item is deleted, there is no way to recover it in the current workbook once your session is closed (until then, it can be recovered using Undo).

Comment: you can add comments for data items from **Field Properties → Comment**, as described in the field properties section. Comments appear to users of the data items whenever they hover over the data item in the Data pane and also from the Describe function.

Edit a comment—
hovering over the data item shows the comment

Describe Sheet: this summary is available from the Worksheet menu to summarize the details of your current sheet. Information includes a description, mark type, data items on shelves, dimension details, measure ranges and data source details. You can easily copy this information to another application such as Microsoft Word by clicking the Copy button.

Sheet Description box

176

Custom data hierarchies

By now, you have seen that Tableau automatically treats date items in your view as a hierarchy, typically starting at *Year* then *Quarter*, *Month* etc. You can go down the hierarchy for more detailed views. In Tableau, you also can add your own custom hierarchies to rapidly navigate your data. Examples include hierarchies for customer, location and product.

The Superstore Sales sample in Tableau has a pre-built custom hierarchy, *Product*, consisting of *Department*, *Category*, and *Item*, which you can see in the Dimensions pane (it is labeled with a flowchart or tree icon). To build your own custom hierarchy, **<CTRL> + click on** *Order Priority* **and** *Ship Mode* **and drag both on top of the** *Container* **item in the Dimensions pane**. This is a little tricky, but when you do it correctly, the Create Hierarchy dialog appears with a default Name of *Container, Order Priority and Ship Mode.* **Change this name to** *Shipping* **and click OK.** The new custom hierarchy appears in the Dimensions pane.

Adding a custom hierarchy in the Dimensions pane

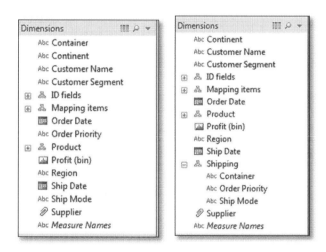

Here is an example of how to use a hierarchy in a view. **<Ctrl> + click on** *State* **and** *Sales*, **click Show Me and accept the default view type of** *symbol maps*. *State* will be on an oval on the bottom of the Marks card (it is now on the Detail button) with a + symbol beside the name. **Click the + symbol and you will see the map detail go from the state level to the city level. Clicking the – sign on** *State* **will remove** *City* **and return to the original level of detail in the view.**

Using the Mapping items hierarchy from Superstore Sales, clicking the + sign on State

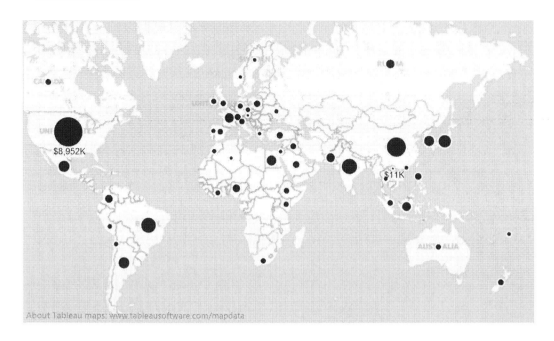

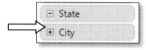

View Data to see the data behind your view

This powerful feature allows you to see a table of all records used in your view. **Select specific data points in your view using <Ctrl> + click, or clicking and dragging over parts of the view, then select View Data (the datasheet icon) from the right side of the hover box that appears.** The dialog box will open. The left tab at the bottom is the Summary tab, which contains summary data based only on the aggregations displayed in the view. The right tab is the Underlying tab, which contains the rows of data behind the selected data items. This feature is particularly useful for examining unusual data values in your view.

Highlight data points and select View Data from the hover box
Summary and Underlying Data in the View Data dialog box

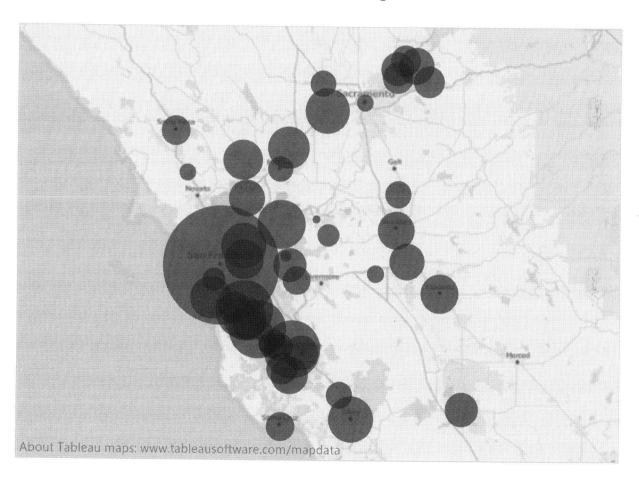

About Tableau maps: www.tableausoftware.com/mapdata

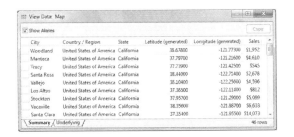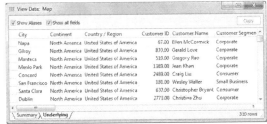

You can resize any field by dragging the side of the header, you can sort by a field by clicking on the header, and you can turn off all other fields not used in the current view by unclicking on *Show all fields*. As you review the data, **you can select rows with click and the <Shift> key, which allows selection of a range of rows, or the <Ctrl> key, which allows selection of multiple specific rows. To select all rows and columns in the dialog, use the square in the upper left of the table (just to the left of the first column header) or <Ctrl> + A.** Once you have selected the desired rows, you can copy them to your Windows clipboard **by clicking on Copy.** You can paste the results into Excel, Word and many other applications, including Tableau!

Bins to divide numeric data items

A data bin enables you to divide a numeric data item into equally sized intervals or "bins". For example, suppose you would like to organize sales transactions into 20 intervals based on sales amount. If you requested to bin sales amount (sales amounts ranging from $0 to $1,000) into 20 bins, Tableau would create bins each having a sales amount length of $50 (e.g., $0-$50, $50-$100, $100-$150, and so on up to $950-$1,000). To do this, you would **right-click on** *Sales* **and select Create Bins**. The Create Bins dialog appears. Unless your data source is very large, typically you would **click on Load** to see the range of values in this field.

The Create Bins dialog for *Sales*
(select Load to see the range of values)

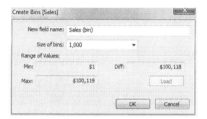

To create 100 similarly sized intervals, **simply divide the difference between the maximum and minimum values (called Diff in this dialog) by 100—in this example, you would use 1,000 after rounding up, so type 1,000 in the Size of bins slot.**

! *Alternate Route:* If you display your data item in a histogram, Tableau automatically bins the item for you.

Bins are very useful for understanding the number of records occurring within each bin (or value range) or examining the total or average value within ranges, as shown in the following examples. In the first chart, displaying *Number of Records*, you can see most transactions are in the first bin and almost every transaction is in the first third of the bins. The second chart depicting *Sales* tells a very different story. The first third of the bins contain the majority of the transactions, however; the remaining bins still have many transactions.

Sales binned and displayed in two views: *Number of Records* **versus** *Sales*

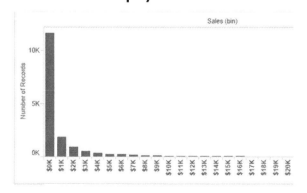
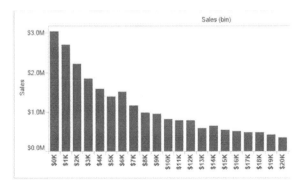

Group dimensions into categories

Tableau allows rapid grouping of selected values from a dimensional item. For example, suppose you want to divide product categories into three groups of roughly equal sales to assign responsibility among three new product managers. In the example below, you can see the categories before and after grouping.

Group *Category* into three similar-sized groups to distribute sales volume among Product Managers

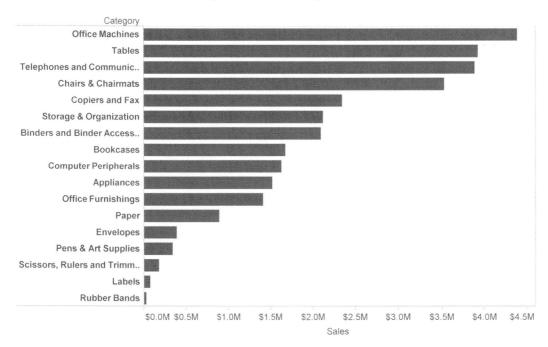

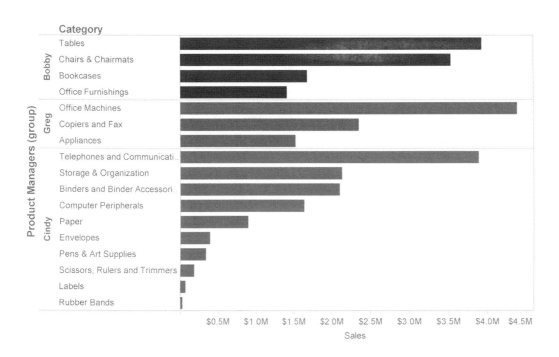

Grouping values directly from the view allows you to leverage the information from other relevant data items. From the view, **select multiple values by <Ctrl> + click or <Shift> + click *on the headers* (not the bars). The paper clip is the symbol for the Group command, and is located in three places: the bottom of the hover box, when you right-click on the group of headers, and on the toolbar. Then, you can rename the grouped values by right-clicking on the header and selecting Edit Alias.** The Edit Alias dialog appears, as shown below. **Type in the new name.**

Rename values after grouping from the view

Note that grouping values from the view automatically creates a new dimension item with the same name as the grouped item, with "(group)" added to the name, and changing the alias does not change the name in the Dimensions pane. **Add Category to the right of Category (group) on the Rows shelf**—this displays the sub-categories included in each group. **Drag Category (group) from the Rows shelf to the Color button,** and your view should be similar to the one shown above.

Additional grouping functionality is available by **right-clicking on the newly created dimension item in the Data Items pane and selecting Edit** so that the Edit Group dialog appears (shown below).

The Edit Group dialog: Group, Ungroup, Rename, and Group "Other" values

All view-based grouping functionality is available from this dialog, along with some additional features. The view-based grouping approach assumes all values of the data item are available. However, if a new value appears in the data after defining the group, it will be ignored unless you specify where to include the "Other" values, a catchall for values not explicitly categorized. You can ungroup values by **clicking on the header and selecting Ungroup. Then drag ungrouped values to an existing group or create a new group by selecting them and clicking Group.** Another powerful feature from this dialog is the ability to find values within the groups by **clicking on Find**, which expands the Edit Group dialog to add a Find sub-dialog area, shown below with all values containing "office" highlighted.

The Find functionality within the Edit Group dialog

You also can create *visual groupings* directly in the view. **Draw an enclosure around the data that you want to include and click on the paper clip that appears in the hover box.** In this example, sales regions were created by visual grouping.

Visually grouping sales regions directly within the view

The power of sets to combine and filter your views

Sets are custom fields that are similar to groups but more powerful because they can be created from one or more existing dimension items. All sets can function as advanced, pre-defined filters or placed on the Rows or Columns shelves as data items. You can have a simple set based on a single dimension item, such as including all order quantities of more than five items. A set based on two or more items behaves as a complex item combining all the unique combinations of the selected dimension item levels in your set. For example, a set could contain all sales amounts greater than $80 with a gross profit greater than $40, or all female customers who shopped at our store before 2012.

Three frequent applications of sets include:

1. Create a subset of one or more dimension items that can be reused in other worksheets as an item with an automated filter based on the levels selected. For example, **click on** *Profit* **and** *Sales* **and accept the default scatter plot on Show Me. Add** *Order Priority* **to the Shape button and** *Customer Segment* **to the Color button**. A chart similar to the figure on the left appears. **Highlight some of the points in the upper right quadrant by <Ctrl> + click. Right-click on a highlighted data point and select Create Set** and the *Create Set* dialog appears, also shown. **Name the set "High value customer segments by order priority" and click OK**. The new set will appear near the bottom of the Data Items pane below Measures in the Set section with the set icon (a pair of intersecting circles) next to it, although you may need to scroll to see it.

Create a set from a scatter plot

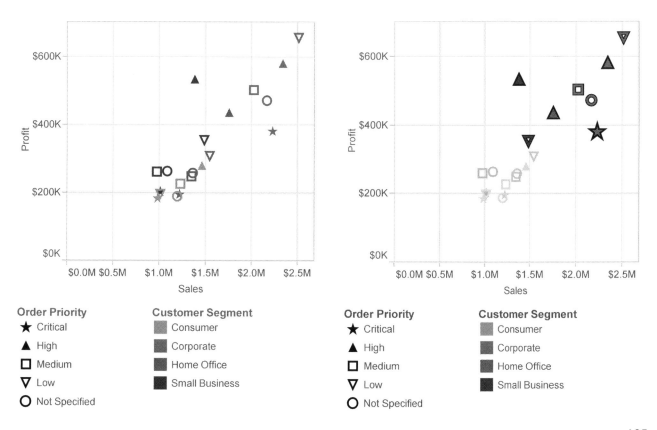

2. Combine two dimensional items into a single item. For example, create a Combined Field using *Customer Segment* and *Order Priority* into a new data item. **Click on** *Customer Segment while holding* **down the <Ctrl> key, click on** *Order Priority*, **and then right-click and select Combine Fields**. A new data item appears, named "Customer Segment & Order Priority (Combined)".

3. Save an existing filter as a set for later use. Using any of the filter functionality, you can reuse the filter in your workbook repeatedly as a set, which is a great time saver! Conceptually, this is very similar to highlighting values from a scatter plot and creating a set. To use this capability, **right-click on a filter on the Filter shelf in your workbook and select Create Set**.

You can use a set similar to any other dimension item. You can add a set to a displayed shelf or to filters.

! *Performance Tip:* Note that if you use a filter and a set based on the same dimension, the result will be what the filter and the set have in common (also called the intersection of the two).

Open a new worksheet. From the set creation examples in this section, **<Ctrl> + Click** on *High value customer segments by order priority* and *Number of Records* and select *text tables* from **Show Me.** A view appears that display the count of records that are part of the Set definition, the "In" records, and those that aren't part of the Set, the "Out" records.

Count of records in and out of set

In / Out of High value customer segments by order priority	
In	8,380
Out	8,418

To see the actual values behind a discrete set (one created using dimensional items like you in the previous section), once you have placed a set on a shelf, **click the drop down on the set item and select Show Members in Set. Then click Analysis → Totals → Show Column Grand Totals.** The view automatically filtered the data, as the set item was automatically added to the filter shelf, and only records that are "In" the set are now displayed (8,380 total).

Members that are in the set

High value customer segments by order priority	
Corporate, Critical	1,236
Corporate, High	1,216
Corporate, Low	1,270
Corporate, Medium	1,178
Corporate, Not Specified	1,252
Home Office, High	870
Small Business, High	718
Small Business, Low	640
Grand Total	8,380

Open a new worksheet. Double-click *Country/Region* **and then double-click** *Sales.* A map of countries with size-encoded values appears. **Click Show Me and switch to** *filled maps.* From the set examples included in this data source, **double-click** *Countries - High Profit & Sales.* **It appears in the Rows shelf by default, separating the view into two maps of the best countries (In) and the rest (Out). On the Marks card, move** *Country / Region* **to the Labels button. Change the aggregate for the** *Sales* **color item from Sum to Average. Finally, right click on the In label on the view, select Edit Alias and change to "Best". Repeat for Out but change to "The Rest".**

Sets as a combination of multiple items and a reusable filter

For more possibilities with Sets, visit www.Freakalytics.com/rgts8 and watch our videos on Better Analytics with Tableau 8. Eight videos are available including two videos about Sets. This video has an accompanying sample workbook so you can follow along at your own pace, if you like.

Chapter 10

Advanced data management in Tableau— Calculated Fields, Functions, and Parameters

---

Chapter Highlights

- Calculated Fields—the power to shape your data

- Functions—keys to powerful calculated fields grouped by data type usage

    o   Numeric

    o   Character

    o   Date

    o   Logical

    o   Type Conversion

    o   Aggregate

    o   Table Calculations

- Parameters—easily adjust your formulas

In previous chapters, you learned the secrets to great data management using Tableau. This chapter will build upon that knowledge by covering advanced topics such as calculated fields and calculated field operators, the many functions available organized in a table for easy look-up, and parameters that allow you to quickly fine-tune the data that you use in your analyses.

Examples in this chapter use both the **Sample—Superstore—English (Extract)** and **Sample—Coffee Chain (Access)** data sources that are included with a standard Tableau Desktop install.

Calculated Fields—power to answer your difficult questions

Sometimes your analysis needs a data item that your original data source does not include, but that you could calculate using the current data items. This is called a *calculated field*. For example, you might need a new data item called *Profit Ratio*, the ratio of the profit field to the sales field. Another example would be the creation of a conditional statement called "Shipping Commitment Met" that determines if the actual time to ship was greater than the promised time to ship, returning a value of 1 if true or 0 if false.

To create a new calculated field, **right-click on an existing data item that you want to include in the calculation and select Create Calculated Field**. The Calculated Field dialog will appear as shown below. This dialog also was shown earlier in the Custom Table Calculation section.

The Calculated Field dialog

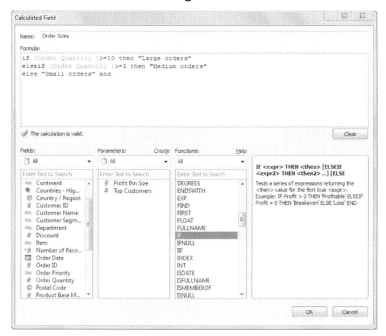

From the Calculated Field dialog, you can name the new calculated field, enter the formula for the new field, add data items from the Fields pane (much better than typing them!), create and use parameters, and find functions by category and add them to the formula. By clicking on an item of interest in the Fields, Parameters or Functions panes, you will see additional details about the selected item in the box to the far right of the dialog. Using fields, parameters and functions, you can create a wide array of simple to very complex calculations to fit a dizzying array of situations.

As you type the formula, text appears, along with a green check or a red "X", just below the formula area indicating if the current formula is "valid". If it contains errors, a dropdown appears to explain your error. Keep in mind that this simply is checking the syntax of your formula, NOT whether the logic you need has been coded correctly! Suppose *orders greater than 10 are considered large orders*, however, you have typed in ">=", *which is greater than or equal to 10*. Obviously, this is an error in your formula, but it is a valid calculation according to Tableau. To verify your formula is functioning as expected, carefully examine your formula results in a separate worksheet. We often use a simple text table!

Here we show an example of validating the formula used in the previous illustration. The new field, *Order sizes*, is used to look at the Number of Records and both the Minimum and Maximum Order Quantity for each order size.

Order sizes	Min. Order Quantity	Max. Order Quantity	Number of Records
Large orders	10	180	11,448
Medium orders	3	9	4,060
Small orders	1	2	1,290

Examining this table, you quickly can recognize the mistake in your formula logic since the *minimum order quantity for large orders is 10*. You can edit the formula **by right-clicking on the calculated data item in the Data pane to bring back the dialog and then changing the first line to read**:

> **if [Order Quantity] > 10 then "Large orders"**

Click OK and now you will see the expected values in your table for the order quantity ranges.

Order sizes	Min. Order Quantity	Max. Order Quantity	Number of Records
Large orders	11	180	10,906
Medium orders	3	10	4,602
Small orders	1	2	1,290

This section contains a detailed list of the Calculated Field Operators and a set of tables that organizes the groupings available in the Functions dropdown from the Calculated Field dialog. Each function includes syntax details and examples using the function.

It is important to note that some functions modify a field (e.g., the left function takes part of the original field and returns it) while other functions test a field or compare fields and return a status back to the calculation (e.g., the length function returns the length of a field while the IF, THEN, ELSE functions check for conditions and returns a value specified by you if true, and another value specified by you if false.)

Calculated Field Operators

To create calculated fields, it is crucial to understand the field operators available in Tableau. The basic operators are shown here in the order of precedence that operator calculations will occur (i.e., multiplication is calculated by Tableau before any addition occurs.)

Operator	Details
*	Used for numeric multiplication: 12*7 will return 84.
/	Used for numeric division: 12/6 will return 2.
+	Addition when used with numbers. Combining or concatenation when used with strings. When used with date fields, it will add the specified number of days to a date: o #June 1, 2009# + 1 will return #June 2, 2009# o " #" marks surround a date value in Tableau (more on this later)
—	Subtraction when used with numbers: o "78 - 10" will return "68". o [Sales] - [Expenses] will return the gross profit from each transaction from a relational data source.

Comparison operators that can be used in expressions:

Operator	Definition	Example
== or =	equal to	1=2 is false
>	greater than	1>2 is false
<	less than	1<2 is true
>=	greater than or equal to	1.1>=(1+0.1) is true
<=	less than or equal to	1.1<=1.2 is false
!= or <>	not equal to	1.1!=1.1 is false

All operators can compare two numbers, dates or strings. They all return a Boolean value, TRUE or FALSE. Note that Boolean values cannot be compared using these operators. For example, FALSE=FALSE is not a valid expression. To compare Booleans with operators, use the logical operators AND or OR. For example, TRUE AND TRUE is valid, returning TRUE. To reverse the outcome of your comparison, use the NOT statement. IF NOT 1=1 ... would return a FALSE result.

In the following tables:

- [Number] refers to any number you type (e.g., 7.8 or -14/3).
- [Item] refers to a valid item from your data source.
- [String] refers to a string you type in (e.g., "Tableau" or "Beauty").
- Singular refers to functions that return the same number of rows as your data source.
- Aggregate categories collapse your data to a smaller number of rows based on your view layout.

Numeric Functions (Singular)

Category	Function	Syntax	Example
Numeric (Singular)	**Round a number** to a specified number of digits.	ROUND([Number],decimal) or ROUND([Item],decimal or [Decimal Item]) decimal is optional, [Number] of decimal places	ROUND(10.47)=10 ROUND(10.47,1)=10.5 ROUND([Height],1)= height rounded for each row in the table
Numeric (Singular)	**Check if a number is null, return 0 if it is or the number if it isn't**	ZN([Number])	ZN(2.1)=2.1 ZN(Null)=0 ZN(0)=0 ZN(Null*2.1)=0
Numeric (Singular)	**Absolute value** of a number or absolute value of each value in a database item.	ABS([Number]) or ABS([Item])	ABS(-10.1)=10.1 ABS(18.2)=18.2 ABS([Profit])=all rows in item as non-
Numeric (Singular)	**Sign of a number**—negative, positive or zero. Negative is returned as -1, positive as 1, and zero as 0.	SIGN([Number]) or SIGN([Item])	SIGN(-3.5)=-1 SIGN([Sales])= sign for each row in the table
Numeric (Singular)	**Square of a number.**	SQUARE([Number]) or SQUARE([item])	SQUARE(6)=36 SQUARE([item])=square for each row in the table
Numeric (Singular)	**Raise a number to a power.**	POWER([Number],power) Or Power([Item],power or [Power Item])	POWER(10,3) = 1000 POWER([LogWeight],2)= weight to the second power for each row in the table
Numeric (Singular)	**Square root of a number.** Returns Null for values of zero or less.	SQRT([Number]) or SQRT([item])	SQRT(36)=6 SQRT([item])=square root for each row in the table
Numeric (Singular)	**Logarithm of a number for a given base.** Returns the exponent needed to raise the base to that number.	LOG([Number],base) or LOG([Item],base or [Base Item]) base is optional, defaults to 10 if not specified	LOG(1000) = 3 LOG([Weight])= logarithm base 10 for each row in the table
Numeric (Singular)	**Natural logarithm of a number.** Returns the exponent needed to raise **e** to that number, or Null if number is zero or less.	LN([Number]) or LN([Item])	LN(7.389) = 2 LN([Weight])=natural logarithm for each row in the table
Numeric (Singular)	**e or Euler's number raised to a power.** **e** is approximately 2.7128 and is commonly used in exponential functions.	EXP([Number]) or EXP([Item])	EXP(2) = 7.389 EXP(-[Growth Rate]*[Time])=**e** to the power of the negative two items multiplied for each row in the table

Character Functions (Modify Items)

Category	Function	Syntax	Example
Character (Modify Values in String)	Remove all left or right trailing spaces only (two similar functions).	LTRIM([String]) or RTRIM([String]) or LTRIM([Item]) or RTRIM([Item])	LTRIM(" Cool ")="Cool " or RTRIM(" Cool ")=" Cool" or LTRIM([Item]) or RTRIM([Item])
Character (Modify Values in String)	Remove all leading and trailing spaces in string.	TRIM([String]) or TRIM([Item])	TRIM(" Cool data ")="Cool data" or TRIM([Name])
Character (Modify Values in String)	Upper case the characters of a string.	UPPER([String]) or UPPER([Item])	UPPER("Stephen 7") = "STEPHEN 7" or UPPER([Name])= names upper cased for each row in the table
Character (Modify Values in String)	Lower case the characters of a string.	LOWER([String]) or LOWER([Item])	LOWER("Stephen 7") = "stephen 7" or LOWER([Name])= names lower cased for each row in the table
Character (Modify Values in String)	Return the 1st n characters of a string (leftmost characters).	LEFT([String],[Number]) or LEFT([Item],[Number] or [Length Item])	LEFT("Stephen 7",3)="Ste" or LEFT([Name],3)= 1st 3 characters for each row in the table
Character (Modify Values in String)	Return the middle n characters of a string starting at a certain character location.	MID([String],start, length) or MID([Item], start, length)	MID("Stephen 7",4)="phen 7" or MID("Stephen 7",4,2)="ph"
Character (Modify Values in String)	Return the rightmost characters of a string.	RIGHT([String],[Number]) or RIGHT([Item],[Number] or [Length Item])	RIGHT("Stephen 7 ",3)=" 7 " or RIGHT([Name],3)= Last 3 characters for each row in the table

Character Functions (Locate Values in String)

Category	Function	Syntax	Example
Character (Locate Values in String)	**Test whether a specified string is within a string.** Returns True or False value. This is a case-sensitive function!	CONTAINS([String], specified string) or CONTAINS([Name], specified string) or CONTAINS([Name], [Specified String Item])	CONTAINS("Stephen","J")= False or CONTAINS("Stephen","eph")= True or CONTAINS([Name], "Eil")= False
Character (Locate Values in String)	**Find the position of the 1st instance of a specified string in a string.** Returns 0 if not found. Can specify starting find character location.	FIND([String], substring, *start*), start is optional, or FIND([Item], substring, *start*)	FIND(" Stephen ","eph")=4 or FIND(" Stephen ","eph",5) =0 or FIND([Name],"eph")=location of 'eph' in each row of a table
Character (Locate Values in String)	**Length of a string.** Includes leading and trailing spaces.	LEN([String]) or LEN([Item])	LEN(" Stephen ")=9 or LEN([Name])= length of name in each row of the data
Character (Locate Values in String)	**Test whether a specified string is at the start of a string.** Returns True or False value. This is case sensitive! Ignores leading spaces.	STARTSWITH([String], specified string) or STARTSWITH([Name], specified string)	STARTSWITH("Stephen ","Jo") = False or STARTSWITH ("Stephen ","St") = True
Character (Locate Values in String)	**Test whether a specified string is at the end of a string.** Returns True or False value. This is case sensitive! Ignores trailing spaces.	ENDSWITH([String], specified string) or ENDSWITH([Name], specified string) or ENDSWITH([Name], [Specified String Item])	ENDSWITH("Stephen ","J")= False or ENDSWITH ("Stephen ","en")= True or ENDSWITH([Name], [Specified String Item])

Date Functions

The following examples use the **#** symbol to surround date expressions. This instructs Tableau to interpret the information between the # symbols as a "Date Literal" and convert it to an internal date value (number) that can be used with addition and subtraction operations.   Some of these functions use date_part, which is constant string argument. The valid date_part values that you can use are 'year' (four digit year), 'quarter' (1-4), 'month' (1-12 or "January", "February", etc.), 'dayofyear' Day of the year (Jan 1 is 1, Feb 1 is 32, etc.), 'day' (1-31), 'weekday' (1-7 or "Sunday", "Monday", etc.), 'week' (1-53), 'hour" (0-23), 'minute' (0-59) and 'second' (0-60).

Category	Function	Syntax	Example
Date **(Create Item)**	**Return the current date or date and time.** Two similar functions.	TODAY() or NOW()	TODAY()=#June 16, 2009# or NOW()=#June 16, 2009 8:10:06 PM#
Date **(Item Calculation)**	**Calculate the difference between two dates expressed in specified increments.** For example, find the number of months between two dates.	DATEDIFF([Date Unit], [Base Date], [Compare Date])	DATEDIFF('month', #July 30, 2004#, #August 1, 2004#) = 1 or DATEDIFF('quarter', #July 1, 2004#, #August 30, 2004#) = 0

Category	Function	Syntax	Example
Date **(Modify Item)**	**Add or subtract a specified amount of date increment(s) to a date.** For example, add 3 months or 3 years to the date.	DATEADD([Date Unit], increment amount, [Date]) [Date Unit] = "day", "week" ,"month", "quarter" or "year"	DATEADD('month',2, #December 15, 2004#) = #January 15, 2005#
Date **(Modify Item)**	**Return just part of the date as a string.** For example, return the month or the year of a date.	DATENAME([Date Unit], [Date]) [Date Unit] = "day", "week" ,"month", "quarter" or "year"	DATENAME('month', #May 15, 2004#) = "May" or DATENAME('year', #May 15, 2004#) = "2004"
Date **(Modify Item)**	**Return just part of the date as an integer.** For example, return the month or the year of a date as a number.	DATEPART([Date Unit], [Date]) [Date Unit] = "day", "week" ,"month", "quarter" or "year"	DATENAME('month', #May 15, 2004#) = 5 or DATENAME('year', #May 15, 2004#) = 2004
Date **(Modify Item)**	**Truncate the date to the start of the unit specified.** For example, truncate a date to the 1st day of a quarter.	DATETRUNC([Date Unit], [Date]) [Date Unit] = "day", "week" ,"month", "quarter" or "year"	DATETRUNC('month', #May 15, 2004#) = #May 1, 2004# or DATETRUNC('year', #May 15, 2004#) = #January 1, 2004#
Date **(Modify Item)**	**Return the day, month, or year of the date as an integer.** These are three similar functions.	DAY([Date]) MONTH([Date]) YEAR([Date])	DAY(#May 15, 2004#) = 15 MONTH(#May 15, 2004#) = 5 YEAR(#May 15, 2004#) = 2004

198

Type Conversion Functions

You can covert the result of any calculation to a specific data type. The conversion functions are DATE, DATETIME, INT, STR and FLOAT. For example, if you want to convert a floating-point number like 12.8 as an integer, INT(12.8) would return 13. Note that a Boolean can be converted to an integer, floating number or a string.

Category	Function	Syntax	Example
Data Type Conversion	**Convert a number or string to a date.**	DATE([Number] or string)	DATE("June 18, 2009") = #June 18, 2009# or DATE(#2009-06-18 18:06#) = #2009-06-18#
Data Type Conversion	**Convert a number or string to a date time.**	DATETIME([Number] or string)	DATE(#2009-06-18 18:06#) = #2009-06-18 18:06:00#
Data Type Conversion	**Convert a number or string to an integer.** Before converting to an integer, the value is rounded.	INT([Number] or string)	INT(1)=1 or INT(-1/3)=0 or INT(1.5)=1 or INT(1.50001)=2
Data Type Conversion	**Convert a date or a number to a string.**	STR([Date] or [Number])	STR(#June 18, 2009#) = "June 18, 2009" or STR(1.05)="1.05"
Data Type Conversion	**Convert a string, integer, or date to a floating-point number.** A floating-point number could be 3.000 or 3.1415.	FLOAT([String] or [Number] or [Date]) Note that there must be no commas or other symbols in the value.	FLOAT(#June 18, 2009#) = 39,982.000 or FLOAT("1.05")=1.05

Logical Functions (If, Then, Else)

Category	Function	Syntax	Example
Logical	**PREFERRED METHOD!** Extended logical test to check whether something is true or false repeatedly and return a specified value. Easiest logic type for most people to read.	IF logical test THEN true value ELSEIF logical test THEN true value ELSEIF repeat many logical tests THEN repeat true value ELSE unknown value END	IF [Sales] >= [Sales Plan]*1.2 THEN "Awesome" ELSEIF [Sales] < [Sales Plan]*0.8 THEN "Disappointing" ELSEIF [Sales] >= [Sales Plan]*1 THEN "Strong" ELSEIF [Sales] < [Sales Plan]*1 THEN "Just Below" ELSE "Unknown" END For [Sales]=90, [Sales Plan]=100 Value returned="Just Below"
Logical	Simple logical test to check whether something is true or false and return a specified value.	IIF(logical test, true value, false value, [unknown value]) [unknown value] is a catch all if the logical test cannot be evaluated, generally due to a NULL in the logical test. Note that it is generally a good idea to use the [unknown value] catchall.	IIF([Profit]>[Budget Profit], "Cool", "Lame", "Huh?") For [Profit]=100, [Budget Profit]=102 Value returned="Lame" or IIF([Items]!=0, [Sales]/[Items], 0, NULL) For [Items]=10, [Sales]=45 Value returned=4.5
Logical	Simple expression checked repeatedly against values to check whether there is a match and return a specified value.	CASE expression WHEN value THEN true value WHEN next value THEN next true value [ELSE catch all value] END	CASE LOWER(LEFT([Company],3)) WHEN "tab" THEN "Tableau" WHEN "fre" THEN "Freakalytics" ELSE "Another company" END

Aggregate Functions

Category	Function	Syntax	Example
Multiple- **Date, Numeric, String** **(Aggregate)**	**Minimum** of two values or minimum of all values in a database item, null values are ignored	MIN(date , [Date]) MIN([Number] , [Number]) MIN([String] , string) or MIN([Item])	MIN(1,2)=1 MIN(Stephen, Eileen)=Eileen MIN([Sales]) = smallest sales amount in table
Multiple- **Date, Numeric, String** **(Aggregate)**	**Maximum** of two values or maximum of all values in a database item, null values are ignored	MAX(date , [Date]), MAX([Number], [Number]), MAX([String] , string), or MAX([Item])	MAX(1,2)=2 MAX(Stephen, Eileen)=Stephen MAX([Sales]) = largest value in table
Any Data Type **(Aggregate)**	**Count the number of rows** in a database item, excludes null rows from count.	COUNT([Item]) Unavailable with Excel, Access, and text files. Create a Tableau extract from to use with these data sources.	COUNT([Sales]) = number of sales rows in table that are not null.
Any Data Type **(Aggregate)**	**Count the number of distinct rows** in a database item, excludes null rows from distinct count.	COUNTD([Item]) Unavailable with Excel, Access, and text files. Create a Tableau extract to use COUNTD with these data sources.	COUNTD([Sales]) = number of unique sales values in table that are not null (if there are 10 sales values but ½ are $5 and the other half are $10, the returned value would be 2.
Numeric **(Aggregate)**	**SUM** of all values in a database item, null values are ignored.	SUM([Item])	SUM([Sales]) = sum of all values in table, null values are ignored.
Numeric **(Aggregate)**	**AVG** of all values in a database item, null values are ignored.	AVG([Item])	AVG([Sales]) = average of all values in table, null values are ignored.
Numeric **(Aggregate)**	**MEDIAN** of all values in a database item, null values are ignored.	MEDIAN([Item]) Unavailable with Excel, Access, and text files. Create a Tableau extract to use MEDIAN with these data sources.	MEDIAN([Sales]) = median of all values in table, null values are ignored.

Table Calculation Functions

Category	Function	Syntax	Example
Table Calculation	**Item number from the first item** in the table.	INDEX()	On the third column of an across calculation INDEX()=3
Table Calculation	**Number of items** in the table.	SIZE()	On the third column of twelve SIZE()=12
Table Calculation	**Distance from the first item** in the table.	FIRST()	On the third column of an across calculation, you are 2 columns past the first location FIRST()=-2
Table Calculation	**Distance from the last item** in the table.	LAST()	On the third column of twelve, you are 9 columns from the last location LAST()=9
Table Calculation	**Running sum, average, min or max** of items in a table.	RUNNING_SUM([Item]) RUNNING_AVG([Item]) RUNNING_MIN([Item])	On the third column of twelve, RUNNING_SUM(SUM([Sales])) = sum of sales in table from columns 1, 2 and 3.
Table Calculation	**Access the table calculation value in the previous item** of the table.	PREVIOUS_VALUE([Item]) If it is the first item, then the expression itself is returned.	SUM([Sales]) + PREVIOUS_VALUE(1) = the SUM([Sales]) on 1st item and Running SUM([Sales]) on 3rd item.
Table Calculation	**Lookup a value from a relative position** in the table.	LOOKUP([Item],Rel pos) Rel pos is an integer to look forward or backwards (negative).	LOOKUP(SUM([SALES]),-3) = the null on 1st item and 1st item value from 4th item.
Table Calculation	**Window sum, average, median, min or max** of items in a table.	WINDOW_SUM([Item], Start, End) Start is start position in table and End is final position for calculation	WINDOW_SUM(SUM(Sales), FIRST(), LAST())=Sum of all values from 1st to 12th item in a 12 column table. AVG, MEDIAN, MIN, MAX also available

Parameters add additional control for your analysis

A few scenarios requested by customers include the ability to: quickly adjust budgeting values up or down in Tableau, dynamically change the number of top states shown in a view, or adjust selection of the percentile shown as the reference line. Parameters enable this type of scenario. Unlike data items, parameters are not part of your new data source, but added by you as needed. Note that the Superstore Sales example has two parameters included.

Using the Coffee Chain sample data source, create a new calculated field from *Budget Profit.* **Name this field** *Budget profit adjusted (2013).*

In the Calculated Field dialog, there is a pane in the bottom named Parameters. **Click the Create link to the right of the word "Parameters" and the Create Parameter dialog appears. Name the parameter** *Profit Target Factor,* **change the Display format to Percentage with 0 decimal points, and change the Allowable values to Range: 0 to 10. Click OK.**

The Parameter dialog

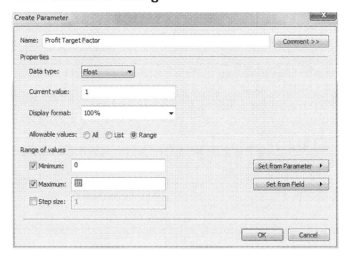

Now you are back at the Calculated Field dialog. **Enter the following formula:**

if YEAR([Date])=2013 then [Budget Profit] * [Profit target factor]
else [Budget Profit] end

Click OK.

Create a bullet graph of *Profit* **vs.** *Budget profit adjusted (2013)* **by** *Product.* **Double-click** *Date* **to add it to the view. Right-click the horizontal axis of the chart and select Swap Reference Line Fields. Click the** *Budget profit adjusted (2013)* **data item at the bottom of the Marks card to select it (it is on the Level of Detail button) and then click the Descending sort from the toolbar. Finally, create a new calculated field: name it** *Exceeds goal?* **and use the formula:**

SUM([Profit]) / SUM([Budget profit adjusted (2013)])

Add *Exceeds goal?* **to the Color button. Adjust the color legend by double-clicking on it, turn on the Use Full Color Range option, click Advanced and Center the legend at 1.**

At the bottom of the **Data Items pane, under Parameters, right-click** *Profit Target Factor* **and select Show Parameter Control.**

Bullet graph by *Product* **and** *Year* **with color highlighting enhancement**

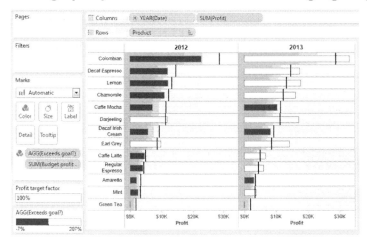

By adjusting the Profit target factor with the slider, you will see 2013 profit targets shift accordingly while 2012 targets remain unchanged (2012 may appear to be changing, but this is due to the adjustment of the *Profit* axis).

Bullet graph with parameter for adjusting targets in 2013

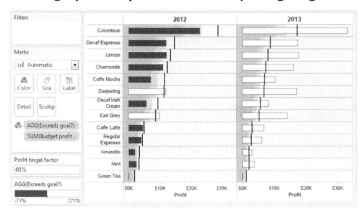

Here are a few more examples of parameters, including use in reference line percentiles and as filter value for selecting the number of top sales states to display.

Parameters in the Edit Reference Line dialog

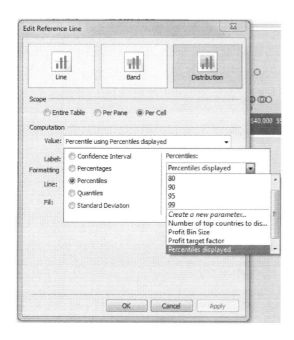

Parameters to control the displayed percentile

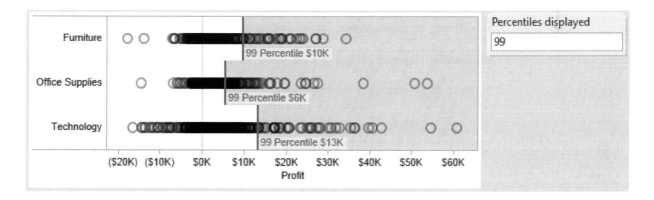

Parameters in the Filter dialog

Parameters to control the number of top countries to display in a map

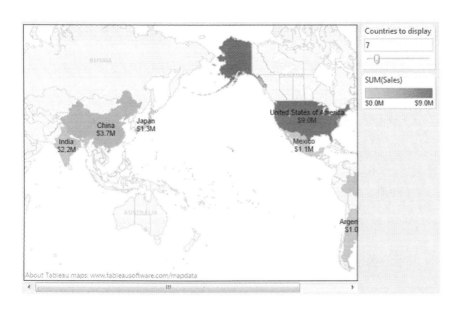

Chapter 11

Advanced data management in Tableau— Managing data connections

---

Chapter Highlights

- Queries—from simple to multi-table data queries

- Data blending—use multiple data sources in one view

- Extracts—accelerate your analysis and work away from the office

---

In this chapter, you will start by creating a new connection to your data, either to a single table or to multiple tables if your data items have been stored separately (all with no SQL required!). Then you will learn about data blending, a feature that allows you to display data from multiple data sources in the same view. Data blending is crucial if your data are stored in more than one type of data system, such as Excel, Access, text, comma delimited files or Oracle databases. This chapter wraps up with Tableau Data Extracts, which are special versions of your data that can reduce query times, enable advanced capabilities and allow analysis of your data when your source database is unavailable.

Examples in this chapter use five datasets. You have used the two data sources that come with Tableau in previous chapters: **Sample—Superstore—English (Extract)** and **Sample—Coffee Chain (Access).** **The other three datasets can be downloaded and saved from the Freakalytics.com website at** http://www.Freakalytics.com/rgts8

1. *The Winery customers and sales* dataset (you may have used this in an earlier chapter)
2. *S and P Ratings* **CSV** data source
3. *Country GDP per Person Euro* **Access** data source

Queries to retrieve the data you need

By default, Tableau automatically connects you with single tables in your data source. Some data sources may contain only one table, while other sources may have many tables to select from and use as data sources. It is beyond the scope of this book to explain how to connect and optimize the multiple data sources that Tableau can connect with—please see the online help from Tableau for extensive coverage of this topic (**Help → Help Topics**).

Connecting to a new local data source in Tableau is easy compared to most applications—if you downloaded and used the winery data in earlier chapters for the Motion Chart or Index function examples, you've already created a new connection. **If not, please download and save** *Winery customers and sales* **from Freakalytics.com at** www.Freakalytics.com/rgts8

On the Tableau Start page, on the main menu, **click Data → Connect to Data**, and a list of data source formats appears. **Choose Microsoft Excel.** The standard Windows Open dialog appears. **Navigate to the location of the Excel workbook of** *Winery customers and sales.xlsx***, and select it.** The Excel Workbook Connection dialog appears. The worksheet names appear in *Step 2: Select the worksheet (table) area to analyze.* **Select Sales data. Keep the default values for Steps 3 and 4 and click OK.**

A second dialog, the Data Connection dialog, appears. It offers three choices: *Connect live* (connects directly to your data), *Import all data* (imports entire data source as a Tableau Data Extract) or *Import some data* (imports a subset of your data as a Tableau Data Extract).

Select the first choice—*Connect live***.** You are now connected to your data! **You can optionally save this data connection as a predefined data source (also known as a Tableau Data Source or TDS file) by right-clicking on the Data Source at the top of the data pane and selecting Add to Saved Data Sources.** If you save the data source to the default location, in your Tableau Repository, it will appear on the home page of Tableau each time you open the application.

The previous example connected to data from only one table (to be technically correct, it was an Excel workbook, so you connected to a worksheet within the workbook). However, Tableau allows you to join two or more tables from your data source using custom SQL (query commands written by you or your helpful database expert) or using the Multiple Tables option.

Explaining how to write custom SQL is beyond the scope of this book. However, there are many excellent books about SQL programming, including ones written for particular databases. Although this book does not cover the details of writing SQL, please note that you can see the generic SQL for the current data connection by **right-clicking on the Data Source at the top of the data pane and selecting Edit Connection → Custom SQL from the Excel Workbook Connection dialog**.

Learning Custom SQL can be very helpful when working with extremely large data sources (more than tens of millions of records) because you can optimize the query execution with your data source based on your workbook needs. Also, consult your database team or data access experts at your company; they may be able to point you to a library of standard queries they have created. Note that query logs from Tableau operations are written in log files located in your local Tableau repository in the Logs directory; this is another potential source of learning more complex SQL statements to fit your analysis needs.

The Multiple Tables option from the *Connect to Data* dialog is also quite powerful. **On the toolbar, click the Connect to Data icon** (the cylinder by itself). **Choose Microsoft Excel and Browse for the**

Sample—Superstore Sales (Excel) data, which most likely can be found in "My Tableau Repository" in your Documents directory. You could use the default data source for Superstore Sales installed with Tableau, but in this example you are manually connecting to it. **Then click on Multiple Tables.** The Connection dialog will change in appearance, shown below on the left. **Notice that you already have the Orders table selected by default, shown below on the left. To add a new table to the data source, click on Add New Table and the Add Table dialog appears, shown below on the right.**

Left—Using the Multiple Tables option for a data connection; Right—Add Table dialog

To add the *Returns* table to the data source, **click on** *Returns*. Optionally, **you can de-select the Table Field Returns$_Order ID** since you do not need this field returned from your query. It only is used to join the Returns table to the Orders table.

Click the Join tab of the Add Table dialog to specify a join path. The join path tells Tableau how the two tables (*Orders* and *Returns*) will be merged together before returning the data source to you. By default, Tableau will use any identically named data item in the two tables to join the data. It also will default to an inner join type, which means only rows that exist with the same values in both tables will be returned. In other words, rows in *Orders* that also do not exist in *Returns* will not be returned for this data source.

If you wanted all rows returned in the *Orders* table and only matching rows from the *Returns* table, you would select a left join instead of inner join. For this example, **select the Join tab, choose Join Type: Left join and click OK** to close the Add Table dialog. **Click OK to close the Excel Workbook Connection, and then choose Connect Live.**

Adding *Returns* to the data source using a left join

Now, you can build a *stacked bars* chart showing how returns differ by customer segment. **Place** *Customer Segment* **on the Rows shelf,** *Status* **on the Color button and** *Sales* **on the Columns shelf** <u>twice</u>**. For the second** *Sales* **item on the Columns shelf, use a Quick Table Calculation to calculate** *Percent of Sales***, and make sure to select Compute using Table (Across). Activate the Labels by clicking on the word Labels on the Marks card and selecting Show Mark Labels.** Since sold orders that were not returned do NOT appear in the Returns table, their status will show up as Null in the color legend. **By right-clicking on the value "Null" in the color legend, you can select Edit Alias to change the alias for "Null" to "Sold"**.

A stacked bar chart of returns (from *Returns* table) by *Customer Segment* as a *Percent of Sales* and *Sum of Sales*

The value "Not Returned" in the stacked bar chart above has been recoded from Null or missing. All rows in *Orders* that did not have a matching Order ID row in *Returns* show the value Null in the data returned from the new multi-table query.

! *Alternate Route:* On the dropdown at the top of the Dimensions pane, click on Tables… the dialog will allow you to add or edit table connections.

One final performance note related to queries. Tableau automatically queries the data source or Tableau extract every time you change the view specification (e.g., changes in marks or shelves). For very large data sources, this can be inefficient if you change your view several times before refreshing the data and must wait for multiple queries to complete. You can toggle the automatic updates feature on and off from **Worksheet → Auto Updates → Auto Update Worksheet or click the toolbar icon (the cylinder with two bars next to it).** If this is turned off, any changes made to the view specification will cause the view to be grayed out until you refresh the data via **Worksheet → Run Update → Update Worksheet or click the toolbar icon (two arrows in a circle).**

Data blending to use data from multiple sources in one view

A common reality for many users of Tableau is that their data is stored in multiple systems, such as Excel, Access, CSV files, Oracle databases and a variety of other database systems. If you have budget data in your Excel data source and actual spending data in Oracle, Tableau allows you to "blend" your data so that you can create a single view that compares budget with actuals.

The following example uses the **Country Blending** data available on the Freakalytics.com web site. If you have not downloaded the two datasets, **go to www.Freakalytics.com/rgts8 Download and save both the *S and P Ratings* CSV and the *Country GDP per Person Euro* Access data sources.**

The first data source is a CSV file containing S&P credit ratings of various countries. The second dataset contains GDP per person in Euros from 1995 through 2009, but only for a subset of the countries in the S&P file. Your objective is to combine country credit ratings with growth rates in GDP per capita.

1. **Connect to the *S and P Ratings* CSV data source. Click the Connect to Data icon on the toolbar, then Text File. From the Open dialog, browse to where you saved the CSV file, click Open, keep all defaults on the Text File Connection dialog and click OK and then Connect Live.**

2. **Double-click on the Country data item**. A map appears with 123 countries displayed, which can be verified by checking the number of marks at the bottom left of the application window. **From the Map Options card, change the top selector from Gray to Dark**. This will make the map nearly black enhancing the contrast of the data items.

3. **Change the Mark type from Automatic to Shape, and place S&P Outlook on the Color button and on the Shape button. Now you can adjust the colors and shapes. Manually sort the order of the ratings in the legends by dragging them up and down from the legend labels.**

The first data source—International S&P ratings

4. **Connect to the *Country GDP per Person Euro* Microsoft Access data source.** Since you were already using data items from the first data source in the view, this data source is automatically linked to it for blending using the data item(s) in common—*Country* in this case. Notice that a link icon is displayed to the right of *Country* in the new data source. There is also an orange stripe down the left side of the data pane to indicate that adding items from this data source in this view will be achieved via blending.

The link icon and orange stripe to indicate blending

5. **Add *Y2009* to the Size and Label buttons.** You will notice that many of the countries have very small data points on the map; this is because they were in the S&P credit rating data source but have no data values in the GDP data source. ***All data blending in Tableau is equivalent to a left join type***. This means that only data item values that are in the data source first added to the view will appear in the view. For example, if the S&P data had no entry for China, but the GDP data had values for China's GDP, China would not appear in the view.

6. **To hide all of the data points that are missing GDP per person values, right-click on the *Y2009* data item oval at the bottom of the Marks card (it is on the Size button) and select Filter. From the Filter dialog, select Special and then Non-null values, and click OK.** The map will now zoom in to display only countries with GDP per person data values.

Display of countries with non-null GDP data

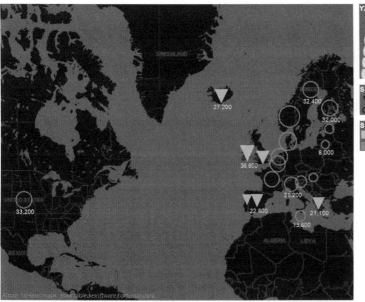

There are two important points to remember about data blending. First, data blending is not part of the data connection definition, it is a behavior specifically activated for a particular combination of data sources. If you create a new worksheet in the above example, you will see that the blending link icon and orange stripe do not appear until you pick an item from more than one data source. Additionally, you can blend using different fields in the different views of a workbook. In fact, Tableau will automatically use only the fields with names in common between the two data sources, so one view could be blending with two data items in common while another view only blends on one data item in common, by default.

Second, if you have data items in common between data sources that are spelled differently or misspelled, you can manually specify how they should be blended (or you could rename the data items so Tableau does it for you!) To demonstrate manual blend specification, **create a new workbook and open the two built-in samples included with Tableau: Sample—Coffee Chain (Access) and Sample—Superstore—English (Extract).**

Suppose you would like to contrast sales in each company over time. **Graph the Superstore** *Sales* **data by** *Order Date* **using Show Me. Then click on the Coffee Chain data source at the top of the data pane.** You will notice that there is not yet a link shown next to any data items in the view (although the orange stripe is visible down the left side of the data items pane). Until you specify a relationship between the two data sources, blending will not occur.

Go to Data → Edit Relationships. The Relationships dialog appears.

The Relationships dialog

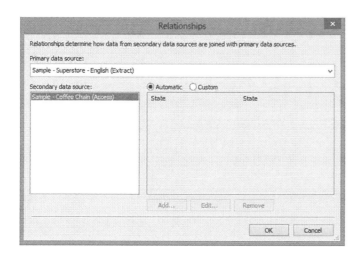
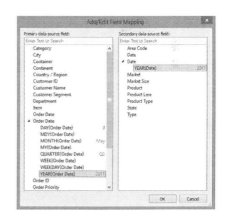

Click the Custom button, select State, and then Remove. Click Add and the Add/Edit Field Mapping dialog appears. Expand *Order Date* **and click on** *YEAR(Order Date)*. **On the right side, expand** *Date* **and select** *YEAR(Date)* **and click OK. Repeat these steps for** *Quarter*. **Click OK to close the Relationships dialog.** You should now see a link next to *Date* in the Dimensions pane—this indicates that *Date* is used to link back from the Coffee Chain to Superstore Sales.

Now that you have linked the two data sources, **double-click** *Sales* **from the Coffee Chain data source to add it to the earlier line chart showing sales by year from the Superstore Sales data. Drill down on the** *Year (Order Date)* **item to show quarters. Click the drop-down for the second** *Sales* **item on the Rows shelf and select Dual-Axis**. Now both data series appear in one row with the two items colored. **Next, edit the alias for the color legend names, changing them to "Coffee Chain Sales" (the color with 8 quarters of data) and "Superstore Sales" (the color with 16 quarters of data). Format each axis based on the color of the series by adjusting the Shading from the format pane, and adjust the axis scale. Finally, filter on the second** *Sales* **item from the Rows shelf, selecting Special, Non-null values.** Note that only eight quarters of data are available between the two data sources with this last change.

Coffee Chain and Superstore *Sales* after blending

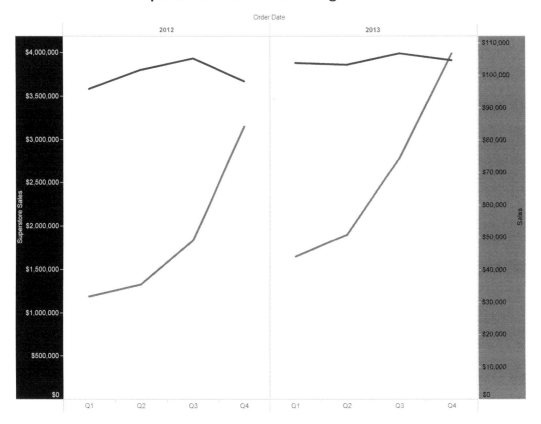

Extracts to accelerate your data exploration in Tableau

A Tableau Data Extract is a special copy of your dataset based on the original source and labeled with the extension ".TDE". You can use extracts to improve query performance, enable certain advanced capabilities and perform analysis when disconnected from your database. Extracts are typically 5 to 100 times faster than file-based data sources and are often 3 to 10 times smaller than local data sources such as Excel and CSV data files. The main disadvantage of extracts is the time required to create them, which typically is limited by the network speed for relational databases or by your local PC speed for building extracts from local data sources.

For a simple demonstration of the power of Tableau Data Extracts, we tested some typical queries with a large 950,000 row Excel data table. This Excel data table had 20 data items based on the winery data that you used earlier in the book, and required 60-80 seconds per query on our laptop. The Excel data file size was 105 MB. Generating a complete extract of this Excel file required 90 seconds and resulted in an extract that was 38 MB in size, a storage reduction of 64%. The big improvement was observed in queries using the generated extract, which typically required 0.1-0.5 seconds. That is 280 times faster! After only two queries, we saved the time that it took to build the extract. We also had a much smaller data source with fast query results for each additional view request.

You can create an extract with or without filters to include only the data that you want in the extract. Extracts allow you to analyze data stored in large data sources that would slow down your work in Tableau (often multi-table joins can take a while with many databases).

You automatically will be prompted to create an extract after specifying a new data source or at any point by **right-clicking on the data source (at the top of the Data pane) and selecting Extract Data**. If you create Extracts via the second method, you can limit extract sizes via multiple methods during the extract specification process.

You also can:

- Use field specific filters, for instance, sales greater than $1,000.00 or state = "Michigan".
- Aggregate data for visible dimensions, significantly reducing the amount of data stored in the extract based on the current non-hidden data item structure. This is very useful if you have 80 dimensions and have hidden all but a few.
- Roll up data based on years, quarters, months, day, hours, minutes or seconds, significantly reducing rows with transactional data—50,000 records in a day becomes just a few.
- Specify that later refreshes of the extract only add new data rather than recreating the entire extract. This is the Incremental refresh option from the Extract Data dialog. In order to use this option you will specify a data field to uniquely specify how Tableau will identify if rows contain new data. For example, with Superstore Sales, you could specify Order Date. This has a big performance boost when querying the source database, since you might have 20 years of data, but a daily update query would only pull a day of data and append it to the current extract.
- Take a subset of the data based on the number of records—percent or specified number of rows.

Please note that the last option is NOT the same as a random sample if your data are ordered by date in the data source, it merely grabs data from the "top" of the data source up to the number of rows specified. In addition, data sources from certain databases such as SQL Server offer the additional capability to select a random sample, which will appear as a third option in the Number of rows area of the Extract dialog.

Creating a new data connection, followed by the Data Connection dialog

Right-click on the data source for the Extract Data dialog
Incremental refresh option shown, using Date to find new rows

After specifying the details of the extract to create, you will need to save the extract to a local file location. Extracts cannot be saved to a network drive for performance reasons. Depending on the size and complexity of your data source and the filters specified by you, extracting data can take a significant amount of time since all of the specified data is retrieved from the data source to your PC. By default, right after you create a new extract, it becomes the data source for the current workbook, until you turn it off (right-click on the data source and uncheck **Use Extract**) which reconnects you to the original data source. Note that toggling the Extract on and off may radically change the data shown in your views if you have added filters or sampling in the Extract data dialog.

You can refresh all extracts in use by your workbook by selecting **Data → Refresh All Extracts**. If you want to remove an extract, right-click on the data source and select **Extract → Remove**. When removing the extract from the project, you will be given the option to also delete it from your hard drive; *do not delete it unless you are certain it isn't in use with other workbooks!*

In summary, the advantages of extracts are:

- When using a file-based data source such as text files, Microsoft Excel or Microsoft Access, extracts radically improve performance.
- Extracts enable additional functionality for file-based data sources, such as the ability to count distinct rows (e.g., how many distinct customer IDs are in the Sales Orders table) or aggregating a measure with the Median function.
- With large data sources (millions or even hundreds of millions of rows), you can improve performance and reduce database loads by using extract subsets (e.g., all records for transactions over $1,000.00.)
- To expedite complex Tableau workbook creation (many views) with very large data sources, you can create an extract with a subset of the data to enable rapid workbook development. Once you have developed the desired views, you can switch to the complete data source by turning off the extract or updating the extract definition.

Chapter 12

Share your insights from Tableau

Chapter Highlights

- Export Images

- Export Data

- Print to PDF

- Workbooks and Packaged Workbooks

- *Tableau Reader*

- *Tableau Server*

- *Tableau Public*

Sharing your work with your colleagues is one way to be more popular! Now that you have created amazing charts and gained valuable insights with your data, you probably are eager to share your results with your managers, co-workers, and customers. This chapter covers many of the ways to share the work you created in Tableau and make it the talk of the town.

Exporting images is quick and painless in Tableau. Additionally, the data used in your view can be exported to several formats. The ability to print your work as a PDF is handy for distribution because PDF documents are accessible with Adobe Reader, a widely used document reader that is available for free on Windows, Mac OS, Linux, Solaris, Android and other devices.

Although saving work created in Tableau is fast and simple with workbooks, you also can embed the data in a packaged workbook if you need to send it to colleagues—they will be able to look at the data behind the views. **Tableau Reader** is a free Windows application that will allow them to open and interact with your packaged workbooks. Tableau Reader includes a subset of Tableau Desktop product functionality. **Tableau Server** is a web hosting product that allows interactive access from a web browser, iPad or Android device with *no installation of software required*. **Tableau Public** is a free version of **Tableau Desktop** for analyzing local data sources and creating analyses and dashboards that you can publish for free to the public domain. You can then share it on your web site.

This chapter uses the **Sample—Coffee Chain (Access)** dataset that is included with Tableau 8.

Export images to other applications

You may need to export your analyses or dashboards from Tableau to Word, PowerPoint or other Windows applications. There are three ways to export graphs from Tableau:

- Windows copy and paste
- Export as an image file
- Print as an Adobe PDF file (this option is covered in a later section of this chapter)

For the most common uses of exporting images, creating a Microsoft Word report or PowerPoint presentation, using standard Windows copy and paste functionality is a fast and seamless route. It will work well unless you require images of extremely high quality.

Copy graphs with Windows copy and paste

1. Select **Worksheet → Copy → Image** or **right-click and select Copy Image** (be careful to click directly on the data in the view and not the headers). The Copy Image dialog box appears. The elements available for selection are based on the view type you are using.

The Copy Image Dialog

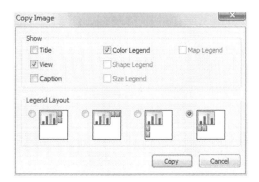

2. Under Show, **select the view elements you want to include in the image**.
3. If you wish to include a legend, **use Legend Layout to determine its location.**
4. **Click Copy**, and the selected elements will be added to the Windows clipboard.
5. To paste a standard quality image of your graph into your Word or PowerPoint document, select **Paste from the Home Menu or the Edit Menu** (depending on which version you have) **or type <Ctrl> + V** (for all versions).
6. For a higher quality graph image, select **Paste Special from the Home or Edit Menu** (depending on your version). **Choose the Picture (Enhanced Metafile) format** to paste a higher quality image into your application.

Export graphs as an image file

1. Select **Worksheet → Export → Image**. The Export Image dialog appears, which is identical to the Copy Image dialog except the Copy button is replaced with the Save button. Once again, the elements available for selection are based on the view type you are using.
2. **Select the view elements you want to include in the image.** If you are using a legend, **choose the Legend Location. Click Save.** The Save Image file dialog appears. **Type the desired file name.**
3. Select the file type to use when saving the graph. There are four file types available.
    a. _PNG (Portable Network Graphics):_ this is the best choice due to the smallest size and best resolution.
    b. _EMF (Enhanced Metafile):_ next best choice, larger than PNG with best resolution.
    c. _BMP (Windows Bitmap):_ third best choice, very large size with best resolution.
    d. _JPEG Image (the default):_ lower quality and moderate file size, not recommended.
4. **Click Save.** The graph image file is exported by Tableau based on your selections.

Use copy or export in Tableau to display views in other applications

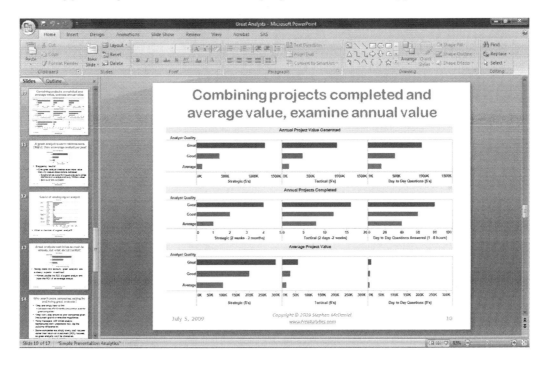

Export data to other applications or back into Tableau

There are several ways to export the data that is behind your view. To export the detailed data *underlying your view* (in contrast to the data appearing in your view) refer back to the "View Data" section in the Data Item management chapter.

A few tips to consider when exporting data from Tableau:
- The data items exported are the data items that are placed on the worksheet shelves. Data items on the Filters shelf are <u>not included</u> unless you also place them on another shelf.
- To include fields without placing them on the Rows, Columns or Marks shelves, **place them on the Detail button on the Marks card.**
- You can select all of the data view to export **using <Ctrl + A>** (Windows Select All), or any portion of the data view by **using the <Ctrl> key and clicking on items or by clicking and dragging.** One exception is copying or exporting to a cross-tab, which always exports all data displayed in the view.

To follow the examples of exports, follow these steps to create this view:
1. **Open the "Sample—Coffee Chain (Access)" data source.**
2. **Click on *Area Code* and *Profit*, and accept the default view in Show Me.**
3. **Add *Market* to the Shape button on the Marks card and adjust the shapes.**

Sample view to use with export examples

222

Copy records to clipboard

This method is useful for pasting records into another application such as Excel or Notepad. You must select part or all of the view to use this method. **Drag over the points in Washington and Oregon to highlight them, and then Worksheet → Copy → Data or <Ctrl> + C**. The records are now available for pasting into another application. Here is what Tableau copies to the clipboard:

Area Code	Market	Latitude (generated)	Longitude (generated)	Sum of Profit
206	West	47.56750603	-122.2772318	$3,823
253	West	47.20133964	-122.4239439	$2,040
360	West	47.03877522	-121.4635792	$1,829
425	West	47.51552986	-121.9352075	$2,017
503	West	45.45323003	-123.2324076	$5,009
509	West	47.34337024	-119.0153828	$1,696
541	West	43.82340572	-120.2964004	$3,378
971	West	45.20118729	-122.7083396	$4,052

Export records to Microsoft Access

This method is useful for large data volumes (greater than 50,000 records) or transferring data to Microsoft Access. With Washington and Oregon highlighted, **go to Worksheet → Export → Data**. The first Export Data to Access dialog appears. **Type a name for the new Access database file or select an existing Access database file**. **Click Save**. The second Export Data to Access dialog appears, as shown below. Note that you can name the table for use in Access, connect to this export after it is created and select whether the entire view or just the selected parts of the view data are exported. **Click OK** to complete the export. If you keep the defaults, the data exported is identical to that found in the above table.

The second Export Data to Access dialog

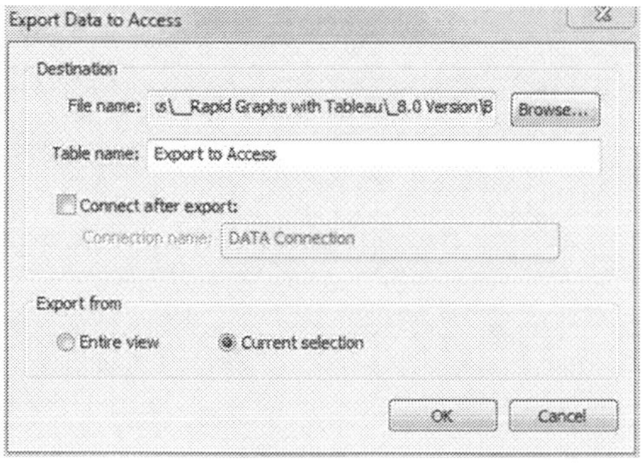

Copy or Export crosstab to clipboard

In the two previous sections, when you copied records from a clipboard and exported records to Access, the data records exported were based on your view selection. These two methods, copying and exporting crosstabs to clipboards, ignore your selections of marks in the view during export. In addition, they both format your export in a simplified version of crosstabs, but the export method has more attractive formatting.

To follow the next two examples, **add** *Product Type* **to the Level of Detail below the** *Area Code* **item** (this information will appear in the view when you hover over a data point). To copy the view data to a cross-tab format, **click on Worksheet → Copy → Crosstab**. The data are now available for pasting into another application, in a format similar to this:

Market	Area Code	Product Type Coffee	Product Type Espresso	Product Type Herbal Tea	Product Type Tea
Central	216	$74	$473	$28	$67
Central	217	$672	$682	$68	$319
Central	224	$225	$455	$405	

The exported table actually has 156 rows, but the table above shows only the first 4 rows for brevity. This simple crosstab format is good for use with other applications beyond Excel.

To export this view as a cross-tab to Excel, **click Worksheet → Export → Crosstab to Excel**. Note that using this method will automatically open Excel, create a new workbook and place the crosstab export in an Excel worksheet. This method is slower than the copy and paste method. In addition, this method does not connect Excel to the data source used in Tableau nor does it place the data in a Pivot Table. An example of the formatting created by this method:

Market	Area Code	Product Type			
		Coffee	Espresso	Herbal Tea	Tea
Central	216	74	473	28	67
	217	672	682	68	319
	224	225	455	405	
	234	240	426	61	511
	262	765	540	960	334
	303	1712	1212	544	459
	309	539	1081	560	389

Again, for brevity, this table has been truncated. Compared to the copy function, the column headers for "Product Type" and the row headers for "Market" are not repeated for each product type or record, respectively, making the table easier to read.

It is important to note that the Export Crosstab to Excel method has much better formatting of the view in Excel than the Copy method. For example, you have to adjust column-widths with the copy method, but the Export method does not require any adjustment and results in a very attractive crosstab.

Print to PDF—export your views to Adobe Reader format

Adobe Reader and PDF files are ubiquitous in both the PC and Mac worlds. In fact, you can also view PDF files on most mobile devices such as iPad, iPhone, Android and other brands. Tableau has an export capability that uses the PDF format as a way to distribute tables, graphs and dashboards created in Tableau. This method of export creates the highest quality images possible, capable of scaling to very large print and display sizes.

To print to a PDF file from Tableau:

1. Use **File → Page Setup** to specify page setup options for each sheet in your workbook, including:
   - What parts of the view to display
   - Show only current page at time of printing (default) versus all pages based on the items placed on the Pages shelf
   - Legend layout
   - Page margins and centering
   - Print scaling, e.g., you can fit to 1 pages wide by 2 pages tall

2. **Select File → Print to PDF** and the Print to PDF dialog appears

Print to PDF dialog

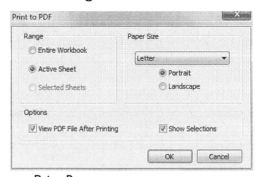

   a. Print Range
      - Entire Workbook—includes all the sheets in the workbook
      - Active Sheet—includes only the sheet currently displayed
      - Selected Sheets—greyed out until multiple sheets are selected
   b. Paper size
      - If you select "Unspecified", the paper size will expand to the necessary size to fit the entire view on a single page
      - Other options are based on Windows standard page sizes
   c. Options
      - Select "View PDF File After Printing" to automatically open the PDF when it is done
      - Clicking on "Show Selections" will highlight selected data points in the PDF
3. **Click OK**. The Save PDF dialog appears.
4. **Choose the location and file name and click Save.**

Packaged Workbooks— bundle your work to take Tableau on the road!

Tableau Workbooks can reference file-based data sources such as Excel, Access, text file or Tableau Extracts. By default, when you save a Tableau workbook as a .TWB file extension, the *connection* information to the data sources is saved in the workbook (but not the data itself). This means that the next time you open the workbook, the views are updated with any changes made to the external data.

In general, saving the workbook with just the connection information is a good route to follow. However, if you need to use the workbook while away from the data source or send it to someone at another organization with no access to your data source, you can include the data, background images, custom shapes and custom geocoding in a special workbook type—the packaged workbook.

Tableau packaged workbooks, which use the .TWBX file extension and have an orange band on the Tableau icon, contain the .TWB workbook, copies of any local data sources, any background images, custom shapes and relevant custom geocoding. Saving the workbook as a packaged workbook also loses any references to the original data sources and images, instead replacing all of these with the packaged sources. Note that the only items included in the packaged workbook are local file based data, such as Excel, Access, text files, Tableau Data Extracts and local database cube files. If you are using a remote database connection, such as Oracle, SQL Server or DB2, you must create a Tableau Extract in order to include these data sources in the packaged workbook.

To save your workbook as a packaged workbook, **click File → Save As** and the Save As dialog appears. **Change the Save as type: dropdown to Tableau Packaged Workbook (*.twbx)**. One big drawback of this approach is that the file size of the actual workbook can grow very large! This is dependent on the size of the data sources being packaged with the workbook. While Tableau uses data compression to minimize the overall size of the packaged workbook, size could still be a problem with data sources in the millions of records or larger.

Packaged workbooks are saved with a different Windows file extension than the standard workbook (.twbx instead of .twb). If you share a packaged workbook with someone that has the same release of Tableau or a later release, they can open it and interact with it, even if they don't have access to the original data sources. One important note: if you share packaged workbooks that contain data from Microsoft Excel 2007 or later or Microsoft Access 2007 or later, you must have Microsoft Excel 2007, Microsoft Access 2007 or the Office 2007 Data Connectivity Components installed on your PC. If you do not have Office 2007 or later on your PC, you can download the data connectivity components from the Tableau web site.

One final technical note, packaged workbooks can be unpackaged (much like unzipping a zipped file) at any time from Windows Explorer. You can unpackage a workbook by **right-clicking on the packaged workbook file in Windows Explorer and selecting Unpackage**. Once unpackaging is complete, you will see the regular workbook file (.twb) and a folder containing the data sources and images from the packaged workbook.

Tableau Reader—share packaged workbooks with your colleagues

Tableau Reader goes beyond static PDF exports to allow anyone to view, filter and explore your workbooks. Tableau Reader, much like Adobe Reader, is a free product that anyone can install in just a few minutes. The application looks and behaves like the full-featured Tableau product for interacting with views from packaged workbooks.

Tableau Reader offers some great capabilities including:

1. View and print workbooks or specific sheets, including annotations.
2. Dynamic interaction with workbooks including:
   a. Sorting.
   b. Filtering from quick filters.
   c. Drilling up and down to change the level of detail in a view.
   d. Rapidly paging through views.
3. Tableau Reader users can copy and export graphics, crosstabs and data for use in other applications.
4. Interact with view and select outlier data points of interest for detailed viewing or export to other applications.

Tableau Reader—freely available, includes a wide range of features for review

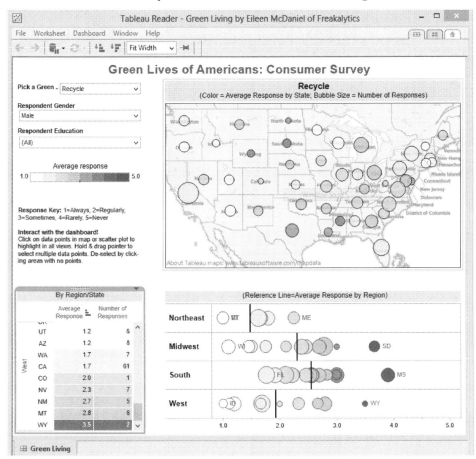

Tableau Server—share your insights with everyone!

Tableau Server is a powerful extension of the Tableau Desktop product covered in this book. It is ideal for teams that need to share live content with a minimum of overhead and a high degree of security. From a web browser, you can use much of the desktop functionality of Tableau across a wide community of users who want to leverage the power of Tableau on the web or on their mobile devices. Installation of software is not required and the content easily can be embedded in Microsoft SharePoint, Wordpress or other content management systems. Web developers will be happy to hear there are a wide variety of ways to embed Tableau Server content with other systems and that Tableau Server even has the ability to be controlled with JavaScript. Tableau Server is ideal for the casual user to consume published workbooks from subject matter experts within their organization.

Among the many capabilities of Tableau Server:

1. Sharing your interactive workbooks created with Tableau Desktop
    a. Anyone with a browser can easily use your work. Supported browsers include Internet Explorer, Mozilla Firefox, Google Chrome and Apple Safari.
    b. Users can leverage up-to-date data with every view.
    c. Seamlessly embed Tableau views into other web applications.
    d. Publish once with Tableau Server specified dynamic data filters based on user permissions. This is very valuable when you have sensitive data that needs to be limited.
    e. Users can extensively edit and use ad-hoc analysis features similar to those in Tableau Desktop. Permissions are used to allow users to access Edit capabilities.

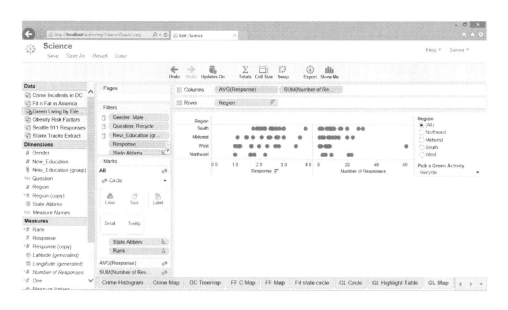

f. Data Sources published from Tableau Desktop can be used on Tableau Server for creating original content.

g. Sort views, and keep or exclude individual data values in your view.
h. Explore the detailed data beneath the view and export data and images.
i. Follow links through a guided analysis path to tell a detailed story.

2. Collaborate across the team
   a. Save your work modifications on Tableau Server for future review by yourself or your team.
   b. All users can add explanatory notes, pose questions and suggested answers or simply contribute an opinion.
   c. Review comments to see the discussion around the data.
   d. Publish elegant dashboards to the web.
   e. Leverage tags to organize your views in multiple ways.

3. Browse the available views
   a. Quickly identify interesting views by browsing thumbnail images instead of searching through long lists of workbook names.
   b. Sort and filter lists of available views to quickly find what you are interested in.
   c. Powerful content search finds precise and related matches. This includes the ability to search the data structure of the views. For example, you could easily find all views that use "Net Profit" in their execution!

4. Embed
   a. Simple embedding of Tableau views in nearly any web apps with standard web links. This method easily provides desired levels of security while widely distributing your analytic information.

5. Schedule
   a. You can schedule Tableau Data Extracts to update to minimize database impact and accelerate analysis from Tableau Server and from Tableau Desktop by using Server refreshed data sources.
   b. You can subscribe to content to receive it by email. This allows easy access to content as the data systems are updated.

Tableau Desktop and Tableau Server

From Tableau Desktop, you can interact with Tableau Server in multiple ways. You can publish to and open workbooks from the server. Workbooks saved to the Tableau Server are centrally available for other Tableau Desktop users in addition to Tableau Server web users.

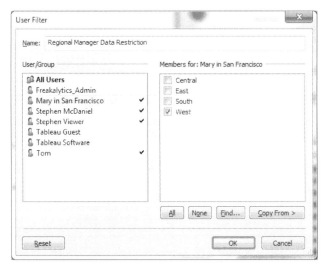

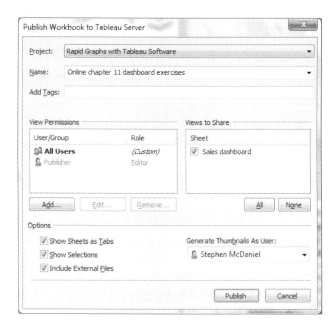

You can import from and publish Tableau data sources to the server. Data sources are available for published workbooks and are synchronized for all users sharing them from Tableau Desktop. This can be a huge timesaver in frequently changing data environments since local data sources do not synchronize back into existing workbooks!

You can specify user or group specific data filters for Tableau Server users. For example, you could allow Tom's dashboard to include data only from the East region and Mary's data from the West region. To use this capability, you first use the **Server → Create User Filter dialog and specify who can see specific parts of the data.** This creates a Set item in the data pane (based on the name of the User Filter) <u>**which must be added to the views in which you need to restrict data access**</u>. Be careful—this feature is for convenience only; address all critical security needs in your database.

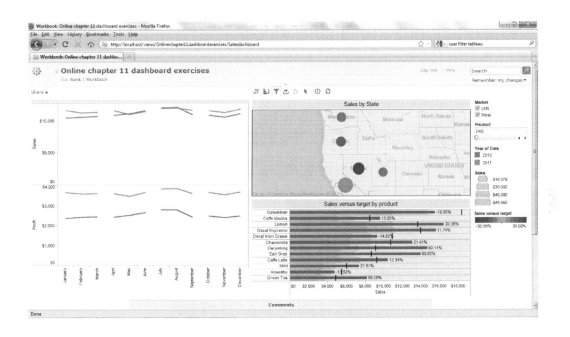

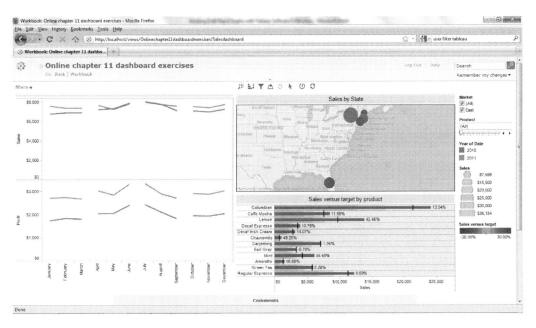

Tableau Public—share your insights with the world!

Tableau Public is a free version of Tableau Desktop that includes Tableau's free web hosting of your work on a simplified version of Tableau Server hosted by Tableau in the cloud. With Tableau Public, you can learn the breadth of Tableau while sharing your insights with the world on any blog or web site. We were excited to have our dashboard featured on the home page of Tableau Public when it launched!

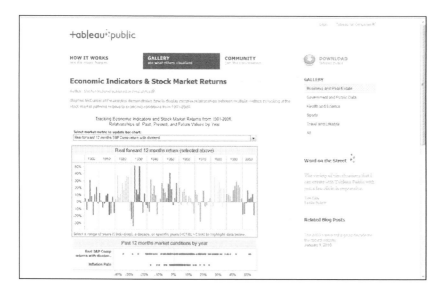

Embedding Tableau Public content is simple and quick. Your web site visitors do not need to install software to view and interact with your published content, since Tableau depends on native Ajax functionality used by sites like Google Mail.

One of the primary restrictions on the Tableau Public desktop application is the lack of remote database connections—instead you can use Excel, Access, CSV and text-based data sources. Additionally, all work you create in this product can be saved only to the Tableau Public web site, hosted by Tableau Software. Remember, this limitation opens all of your work and data so *they are visible and fully accessible to the public*. Finally, Tableau Public has size limitations for the total amount of project storage available to your user account (currently 50 MB, approximately 20 to 80 workbooks, and no more than 100,000 rows per data source).

Publishing to Tableau Public can occur only with projects that use Tableau Data Extracts, since this minimizes project sizes when published while optimizing performance. You can publish from Tableau Desktop in addition to publishing from Tableau Public desktop—**go to Server → Tableau Public → Save to Web (As).** You will need a Tableau Public user account and password to publish your first workbook on Tableau Public. Finally, once the workbook is published, you will see options for e-mailing the workbook and a separate option for embedding the view on your blog or website. Visit our gallery of examples at www.Freakalytics.com/examples

Appendix #1—Timesaving Tips

Valuable keyboard shortcuts

Keys	Action performed by Tableau
<Ctrl> + A	Select all data in view
<Ctrl> + C	Copy selected data
<Ctrl> + D	Connect to data source
<Ctrl> + E	Describe Sheet
<Ctrl> + F	Activate the find command in the Data window
<Ctrl> + H	Switch in and out of Presentation Mode
<Ctrl> + M	New worksheet
<Ctrl> + N	New workbook
<Ctrl> + O	Open file
<Ctrl> + P	Print
<Ctrl> + S	Save file (typically the workbook)
<Ctrl> + V	Paste clipboard
<Ctrl> + W	Swap rows and columns
<Ctrl> + X	Cut selection
<Ctrl> + Y	Redo undone action
<Ctrl> + Z	Undo last action (can be used repeatedly)
<Ctrl> + (Left)	Narrow view rows
<Ctrl> + (Right)	Widen view rows
<Ctrl> + (Down)	Shorten view columns
<Ctrl> + (Up)	Lengthen view columns
<Ctrl> + 1	Show Me! Dialog
ENTER	Add last selected data item to the worksheet
F1	Help
<Ctrl> + F4	Delete the current worksheet or hide it if used in a dashboard
<Alt> + F4	Closes the current workbook
F4	Page forward playback—starts and stops playback of pages shelf
F5	Refresh the data source
<Ctrl> + .	Page forward one page—skip forward one page based on pages shelf
<Ctrl> + ,	Page backward one page—skip back one page based on pages shelf
<Ctrl> + Tab	Cycle through the worksheets in the open workbook
<Shift> + F6	Select mode—selects objects in view
<Shift> + F7	Pan mode—mouse pointer plus dragging moves elements in view
<Shift> + F9	Zoom mode—mouse pointer plus dragging zooms in view
F9	Run query for current view definition
F10	Toggles Automatic Updates on and off—useful for larger data sources
F12	Reverts workbook to last saved version

Select Marks and Pan and Zoom in a View

Using the left mouse button, you can perform a variety of mark selection activities:

Keys	Action performed
<Click>	Selects an individual mark w/o retaining prior selection(s)
<Drag>	Selects a group of marks w/o keeping prior selection(s)
<Ctrl> + <Click>	Adds or removes individual marks to the prior selection(s)
<Ctrl> + <Drag>	Adds a group of marks to the prior selection(s)
<Shift> + <Click>	When over a view, the <Shift> key immediately changes the mode to pan (pan moves the entire view)
<Double-Click>	Centers and zooms in, only shows nearby data

The Zoom Controls

Zoom controls appear in the upper left corner of your view when requested. The one exception is maps, where they automatically appear.

To toggle the control on or off, **Right-click over the view and select Show Zoom Controls or Hide Zoom Controls**.

Keys	Action performed by Tableau
<+ on Zoom Control>	Zooms in at the center of the current view location
<- on Zoom Control>	Zooms out from the center of the current view location
<Box + on Zoom Control>	Drag the left mouse button to zoom in on an area
<Pushpin on Zoom Control>	Releases all zooms and panning, resets the view to all data

Appendix #2—Build a Basic Dashboard

We've taught entire courses on how to design and build dashboards in Tableau over multiple days, so the topic can be quite complex. In this section, you will learn the basic functionality so you can get started. For more advanced dashboards, visit www.Freakalytics.com/examples.

Dashboard Audience

VP of Sales at a cheese maker that sells to the public and to gourmet retailers

Overall Objective of Dashboard

Sales updates for monthly review by Sales Vice President (VP)

The Sales VP has four questions:

1. What are sales by state?
2. What were sales by customer contact method in 2013 compared to 2012?
3. What are the actual sales by item versus the target sales?
4. What are the actual sales by customer contact method versus the target sales?

Download the Cheese Factory sales data packaged workbook from www.Freakalytics.com/rgts8d

Included in the workbook:

- Data source contains two years of sales data for 2012 and 2013.
- Four worksheets with views answering the four questions above.
- The final dashboard is illustrated at the end of this appendix.

Build the dashboard

Open the workbook, and in any one of the worksheets, on the main menu, select Dashboard → New dashboard. In the Dashboard pane on the left side, double-click on each of the four worksheets in the numbered order. Also in the Dashboard pane, in the Dashboard Size section at the bottom, change Desktop to Automatic so the 4 views fit within the workspace. The worksheets are arranged in the order added and the legends for Q1 and Q2 are on the right.

Adjust containers

Dashboards are comprised of containers that contain the views, legends and filters and are outlined by solid lines when you click on them. First, move the legends to the left side of the dashboard. Click on the white space under the legends and a solid dark blue container will appear along with hatch marks in the empty space. Hover at the top of the container on the dotted area to bring up the four-way arrow, and drag and drop the container to the left side of all 4 views. It can be tricky to drop the container in the right place, so you may need to practice.

You can resize any container by hovering over its edges and using the double-sided arrows. Also, depending on your screen size and computer settings, there may be scroll bars in your views. To remove them, click on the view so that the container appears, and use the dropdown on the upper right of the individual view to select the **Fit** option.

Create actions

You can create **actions** to give the user or reader the control to select specific data by a mouse-click, right-click or hover. In this section, you will learn about filters, highlighting and the actions summary.

Filters are frequently the most important action on a dashboard! The four main uses of filters are relative dates, quick filters, multi-sheet filters and using views as filters. The first three are Filters that can be created by dragging data items to the Filter shelf. The last one is an Action Filter. Note that Action Filters are different from Filters/Quick Filters, so keep this distinction in mind. Additionally, if you have the same data item in play with both Filters and Action Filters, this can cause unexpected results.

Filters

1. *Dates:* Both years of data are shown in each view. This is correct for Q2, but Q1, Q3 and Q4 should show relative date by year (relative to today). Since this is fictional data, you'll use 2013. Use *Go to sheet* arrow (square with arrow at the top right of the sheet). If you are reading this in 2013, pl0ace Date on the Filter Shelf → Filter Field [Date] → Relative date → Next → Years → This year → OK. Note that in the real world, you may have to choose *Previous year or even adjust Anchor year, which you would rarely do with live data in your business*. So Q2 matches the other views, click on the color legend to change 2013 to blue. Click again on the color legend to release the selection.

2. *Quick filters:* Quick filters are the best way to give the user control. These are "Local", which means that the default operates only on that particular view. On the Q2 dropdown, Quick Filters → **Contact method**. The filter appears in the left container. De-select (All) and Q2 disappears. Now select Email, and Q2 re-appears, but the other views will not update.

3. *Global filters:* Global filters operate on all views for a given data source. Use the dropdown on the quick filter for **Contact method** → Apply to Worksheets → All Using This Data Source. Now all the views update.

4. *Views as Filters:* On Q3, use **Item name** as a filter. On the dropdown menu, select *Use as Filter*. Click on **Petaluma Pear** —the other views will update. Press *Escape (esc)* to release selections, but note that quick filters aren't affected. Check (*All*) on the **Contact method** quick filter.

Highlighting

On Q4, click on **Newsletter**, label or bar. Use the **Highlight button** on the far right of the toolbar to turn on highlighting by **Newsletter** by selecting **Contact method** from the menu. Highlighting **Newsletter** causes "gray-out"—other contact methods totally gray out.

Actions Summary

On main menu, select Dashboard → Actions. This displays any actions that you generated by using a menu, so quick filters aren't included. It lists the filter in Q3 and highlighting from Q4.

Screenshot of final dashboard

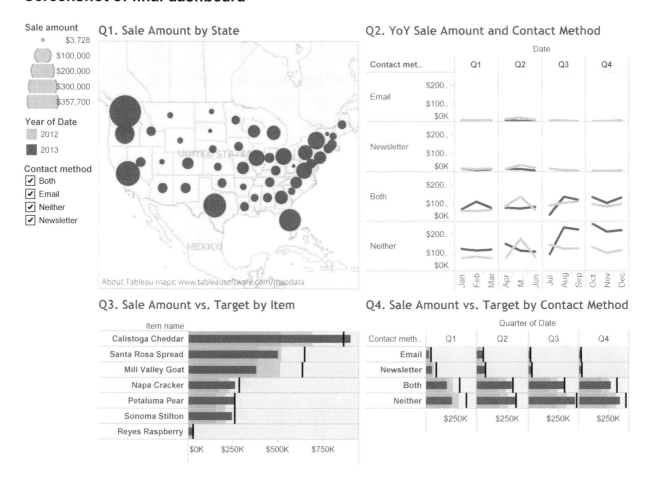

Visit us at www.Freakalytics.com/rgts8 for a video that reviews major dashboard functionality. This video has an accompanying sample workbook so you can follow along at your own pace, if you like.

Index

24330889R50132

Made in the USA
Charleston, SC
19 November 2013